In China with Green Day

Aaron Cometbus

In China with Green Day

ISBN: 979–8–88744–138–2 (paperback)
ISBN: 979–8–88744–139–9 (ebook)
Library of Congress Control Number: 2025931219
Interior design by briandesign

10 9 8 7 6 5 4 3 2 1

PM Press
PO Box 23912
Oakland, CA 94623
www.pmpress.org

Printed in the USA

1

WHAT HAPPENS WHEN friends grow up together but make choices that lead them down fundamentally different paths? Can they still travel together despite their differences? That's what I wondered as I boarded the plane bound for Thailand and, for the first time in my life, took a seat in first class.

Nearly twenty years had passed since I'd last toured with Green Day, and much had changed in that time. Then I'd been the only roadie, or one of two. Now they traveled with bodyguards, caterers, a tailor, and a pyrotechnics expert. For this Asia tour, they had a seventy-person crew—slimmed down from the usual two hundred—and none of them were roadies in the traditional sense. The loading of equipment and selling of T-shirts was all contracted out to professionals, most of whom they never met.

Obviously, Green Day had changed from their days as a small punk band in an Econoline van. Now they were something too big and weird to comprehend. I had changed too, but in ways that were not as readily apparent. To the stewardesses I still looked like a roadie, which is to say unshaven, disheveled, and covered in hickeys, with a pinned-together backpack full of dirty socks. I was muttering to myself, too—a little mantra that went like this:

"Don't be judgmental, don't be difficult, don't be self-righteous. Just go with the flow and enjoy the ride. Don't be judgmental, don't be difficult, don't…"

Because, you see, I hadn't changed that much. Not enough.

I was determined, for once, to be a good guest: someone who eases tensions and tempers instead of inflaming them. I'd made a career of stepping into other people's lives and comparing them—usually unfavorably—to mine. The fact that Green Day had invited me to share their world for two weeks was especially generous because they knew we didn't always see eye to eye. Not only did they invite judgment by bringing me along, they practically insisted on it. Mike said that if I came along on the trip, I had to write about it.

I thought about my other old friends. How many would bring me into their world even for a night? They might have me over for dinner, but more often we ate out. If I was visiting from out of town, I might crash on their couch—though it was better and easier most of the time to stay at someone else's house.

My old friends had new families and new lives, and tensions tended to flare up when someone entered the picture who they'd known in a different time and place. How many jealous husbands and wives had I faced, and kids resentful of the intrusion—angry that the attention they usually received was given to a stranger instead?

Old friendships were difficult to explain. Their histories were complicated and often messy, rife with landmines which could still be easily set off. That was something I didn't blame my friends for wanting to avoid. My personal life was fragile, too, and didn't always sync up with the past or bear scrutiny from outside eyes.

Between me and Green Day, all those factors applied: the old tensions, the crossed wires, the jealousies, the buried landmines. On top of it all was their success and fame, which made *everything* weird.

Yet they had offered to bring me into their world anyway, not just for a night but for a full two weeks. Old friendships are fragile and valuable but don't need to be kept in a museum—that's what they seemed to be saying. And because I couldn't share this part of their world otherwise, they were paying my way.

Funny, though: I didn't realize that they weren't the only ones laying themselves bare—not until I took my seat on the plane.

I would have to get used to the invasion of *my* privacy. I, too, would be scrutinized.

A voice cut into my thoughts. It was Mike, standing next to me.

"I detect the scent of soap," he said, flexing his nose.

"The new Aaron!" That voice was Tre's—and if there'd been any doubt, the high, whinnying laugh that followed cleared it up.

If a roadie in first class had raised any eyebrows,

they were aimed elsewhere now. Green Day's rhythm section was even louder offstage than on. Their arrival in the aisle turned every head on the plane.

In his Chinese pajamas, Mike looked like a Buckingham Palace guard or a member of Sergeant Pepper's Lonely Hearts Club Band. Tre sported a hot pink tracksuit that was a few sizes too large. Dressed for maximum comfort for the all-night flight, both wore fuzzy slippers and had padded blinders to cover their eyes.

No one would be staring at *me* on this trip, I realized.

Billie, the third member of the trio, had always been quieter in demeanor as well as appearance. Sitting in front of me, he was not particularly noticeable: a sleepy cholo. Besides the back pocket comb, he still dressed like he had in the sixth grade, in the style of his hometown's Latino gang—Sugar Town Barrio, named after the city's sole industry. Even when Green Day hit it big, Billie's first instinct was to buy a lowrider bike with a padded steering wheel. The mansion was an afterthought.

Welcome to the conflicted world in which I was a guest.

Much to my surprise, Mike and Tre scooted in next to Billie and took a seat on either side. It was one thing to be a successful band still on speaking terms—unheard of, really—but quite another to choose to be right next to each other, especially on a long and uncomfortable flight. Rather than rockstars, they looked like sweethearts on a long-awaited trip, or kittens in a cardboard box outside the co-op. Watching from behind, I felt like I was in the loft of the old van. They seemed closer now than they had ever been.

That was what struck me right away: not how much things had changed, but how much they were eerily the same. Touring in a jumbo jet was certainly different from waking up in a field outside Philly with a gun to your head, to give just one example from the first Green Day tour. Yet the ridiculousness, the surrealness, and even the exciting sense of danger was the same. Now it was crazed fans at the airport who tried to kill us, not cops. And the last time the police stopped me and Billie, it was to ask for his autograph.

Ugh.

Yes, everything had changed and nothing had changed. Billie seemed the same as he had as a teenager, alternating between dotingly sweet and stormily sullen. Tre and Mike were still goofy, competitive, and hungry for attention.

Once upon a time, they'd looked up to me as a wise elder, but by our third tour together I'd come to seem more like a nagging in-law. That was inevitable; after all, it couldn't be easy traveling with someone who was always right.

And where would they be today, if only they had followed my advice?

Washing dishes, probably. And miserable, like most of our old friends.

Yeah, that was the kicker. Signing to a major label

was kind of a dumb thing to do, but it turned out to be a great decision for them. Now I was enjoying the rewards from the move that I'd been first in line to tell them *not* to make.

They'd been demonized, ostracized, and ridiculed while I enjoyed my moral high ground and played it safe. Then, after twenty years, when the coast was clear, I emerged from my cave and got on the plane. After two decades of nothing but bagels, I was hungry as hell. First I devoured a whole braised salmon with carrots and kale and caramelized leek. Then I ordered a gelato, an espresso, *and* a cognac. That, it turned out, was only the appetizer.

"Here is the dinner menu," said the flight attendant as she came around passing out warm towels.

Could you really have it both ways? This was too good to be true.

Don't get me wrong: there's nothing wrong with washing dishes—and feel free to tell my roommate that. The happiest person I know does it for work. He puts in his eight hours, then goes home and reads a book from cover to cover. He is elated and "living the dream" because that's exactly what he wants from life, nothing less or more.

But the Green Day guys were different. They had a special talent and a burning need to share it. Mike's restless energy was wasted gutting fish for minimum wage, as was Billie's every time his mom made him rake the yard. He had to get every last leaf before she'd let the band use the living room to rehearse—I remember the long wait. No doubt about it: stuck at dead-end jobs, their passion would have festered and turned to bitterness.

I thought of our mutual friends who were brilliant artists, writers, and musicians. I never doubted that they would all become famous in their separate fields. Instead most of them petered out, either from a lack of success or a lack of belief in themselves—or from too much of either one. It wasn't their lack of fame that was sad to me, but the fact that they'd completely given up on their creative work.

Green Day had not only fulfilled their potential, they had far exceeded it. They had overcome obstacles and refused to quit. They had gotten better and better *because* of what they faced, not in spite of it. Maybe that was why they still enjoyed each other's company: who else could understand what they'd been through?

They had made an all-or-nothing, make-or-break gamble, and won. That was old news. But like most "all-or-nothing" decisions, there was a high price to pay: their lives were ripped right out at the roots. Even decades later, they still seemed wounded from being shunned by the punk scene which they'd been part of and loved.

And the scene itself? It had never really recovered or been the same, though we all liked to pretend. It had gone so far underground that sometimes it felt like our heads were buried in the sand.

I'd been to Green Day's big concerts and seen the look of pure joy on the faces of their fans. I'd felt it myself. It made questions about major labels and punk taboos seem academic. It transcended all the hype, the high ticket price, and the alienating aspects of a big rock show—and that was a lot to get past. There was nothing alternative about it, yet the audiences left the concerts happy and relieved. At the DIY shows I championed, the showgoers often departed looking more lonely and forlorn than when they'd arrived. The contrast was impossible to dismiss.

But were the band members themselves happy? Had success given them what they wanted? That was harder to gauge.

The lives of the Green Day guys were very different from mine, but so what? I wasn't desperate anymore to convince everyone to think or live exactly like me. In fact, I was grateful for our differences. I was thankful that we had made different choices in life and taken diverging paths.

"That's what friends are for," I thought as I began to drift off. "They offer us windows into worlds we wouldn't otherwise get to see. We can experience the roads not taken, vicariously."

2

I BOUGHT A CAMERA for the trip, a little disposable point-and-shoot thing. Unfortunately, the photos came out looking like crap.

Here's what you would get if I'd been properly equipped:

Photo One: Green Day and their entourage being led through a shopping mall, surrounded by a phalanx of bodyguards and Thai police. "Bangkok looks more mall-ish than I remember," Billie sighed.

That was our official welcome to Bangkok, annoying but not so different from what I'd experienced on other tours after making the mistake of letting some self-appointed ambassador show us around. The difference here was that strangers would suddenly be at my side trying to blend in, walking and talking with me as if we were old friends. Then the security would spot them and swat them away like flies. It was disconcerting because I longed to talk with some locals, but these overzealous Green Day fans gave me the creeps. They didn't seem to see the band as human beings. There was something fanatical about their fandom. It wasn't hard to imagine one of them pulling out a gun.

I felt torn. My instinct was to protect my friends, yet I realized I should leave that job to the bodyguards. Punch a pestering fan, and Green Day would soon have a million-dollar lawsuit on their hands.

My role as roadie and friend had also been to think outside the box—to suggest, as I did in the Bangkok mall, that we explore the parking lot or roof instead.

The bodyguards looked at me as if I were insane. Was it they who didn't understand Green Day, or was it me?

Photo Two: Green Day in a tuk-tuk, one of the little three-wheeled Thai taxis that resemble souped-up and overdecorated golf carts. Two limey photographers were along on the tour, working on a coffee table book on the band, and this was but the first of many dumb ideas for photo-ops they had. Crammed into the tiny car, Green Day looked like carnival clowns, or a scene from *A Hard Day's Night*. With these photographers, the band's image was bound to get even more constricted than it already was: either foolishly wacky or like constipated-looking James Deans.

Feh! The real Green Day was more nuanced and interesting. The limeys got on my bad side right away by taking pictures of limbless beggars without asking permission or putting anything in their cups. Besides, they talked too loud and too much.

Photo Three is two wildly gesticulating limey photographers shitting bricks as their tuk-tuk driver misses a turn and rides off into the sunset.

Photo Four is three massive, neckless bodyguards

and a couple of monstrous Thai pigs flying into a panic as their overstuffed tuk-tuk gets caught in traffic while the band's vehicle drives off unattended.

This is where the fun begins!

Photo Five is me lying across Green Day's lap after taking a flying leap into the window of their tuk-tuk from the one carrying me and their road manager, Bill Schneider. The driver—urged on by Tre—is doing wheelies, which nearly cause us to capsize.

The tuk-tuk stalls, but Schneider, resourceful as ever, pulls up and manages to fix the engine with what looks like a combination of peanut butter and chewing gum. He was characteristically evasive later when I pressed him for the formula.

Soon we were off again, but by then it was too late: the photographers and bodyguards had caught up. Ten eyes and two necks glared at me for being in the way.

I got the message. The easiest way to get along with everyone was to blend into the scenery—or better yet, to disappear entirely. I hadn't gotten a chance yet to really talk to Billie, Mike, or Tre, but there would be plenty of opportunity for that in the weeks ahead. In the meantime I wanted to be careful not to crowd them. This was a perfect time to split off and see Bangkok for myself.

At first I kept the city at arm's length, staying on major roads so as to not get too badly lost. I eyed all the delicious-looking food stalls, but forced myself to pass, remembering the dire warnings of a nurse friend back home who happens to be a bit of a hypochondriac.

Then I dove in headfirst. I tried any food I couldn't readily identify. The carts parked along festering, stinking canals were the tastiest, and one perched atop a heap of rubble in what looked like the city dump. I kicked away the rats that came up to sniff at my feet. They eyed me angrily and scampered off to drink from puddles of piss in the street. If only I'd had the foresight to get flu shots like everyone else on the tour!

I got into the swing of things pretty fast, shouldering through narrow alleyways and dodging people doubled up on bikes. When one alley inexplicably dead-ended into a dining room, I profusely apologized to a family of Sikhs. Alleys here were just as likely *not* to be thoroughfares, I realized.

Walking around with Green Day and their bodyguards, it was impossible not to create a spectacle. Walking around by myself, I felt invisible and at ease. That never would have been the case if I'd arrived in Thailand on my own. The awkwardness of their fame had broken the ice, and had the unexpected effect of making me feel completely comfortable in an unknown country alone.

My senses were tingling from the array of new sights and sounds, but no matter how intoxicating it was to be in Asia for the first time, it was nowhere near as foreign as the world of Green Day.

I felt more or less at home, which came as a surprise, because on previous trips abroad I'd been completely ill at ease. Cultural misunderstandings and an inability to communicate had landed me in painful and even dangerous situations in Europe. As a result, I'd pretty much given up on traveling overseas.

I had assumed my alienation would be even worse in non-European countries, though my wonderful experience in Istanbul on a previous tour should have tipped me off. Perhaps it was Europe itself that made me feel out of sorts.

No one I encountered now seemed threatening, or threatened by me. The only attitudes I received were curiosity or bemused indifference. Europe had felt oppressively xenophobic in comparison.

For the first time ever, I wasn't desperately searching for a safe place to rest my head or stash my bag; that probably helped. Those concerns had dictated almost every aspect of my previous trips, and taken up most of my energy.

I didn't have to talk to anyone or try to cross cultural and linguistic divides. Communication was one of the greatest pleasures of traveling, yet I was glad to bypass that challenge for once in my life. Walking through unknown cities wasn't the best way to meet people, anyway—take it from an expert. I'd traveled through the US for twenty-two years, and even walked across it once, and only made friends with one complete stranger, a girl I spent the day with in Omaha.

Oddly enough, I didn't get lost in Bangkok, though my map was of tourist traps, showing only what to avoid. The poorer quarters were just blank spaces on the grid, as if wishful thinking could make them go away. When I'd asked the hotel clerks for directions before heading out, they'd taken great efforts to dissuade me from my route. They'd even summoned a coworker more fluent in English who cautioned me as one would a child, as if the whole thing was a misunderstanding on my part.

"Don't take the water taxi under any circumstances," she scolded. "Very dangerous. Bad diseases in the water, sir. Wait right here, we have called you a car. Do *not* leave!"

Photo Six, had it been taken properly, would show a thin, flimsy boat piled high with passengers, one of whom, in traditional roadie garb, is helping hold up a giant canvas screen to keep the waves of festering, malarial water from crashing in on all sides.

By the time the boat got across town I was soaked, but the sun shone down warmly on my wet clothes.

What good is ignorance if you can't use it to break a few rules? Half a block from the water taxi stop, I heard plastic sandals slapping against the sidewalk—the sound of someone running to catch up. Luckily, it wasn't the skipper demanding the fare I'd skipped, but the old woman I'd sat next to on the boat, who'd volunteered directions to a nearby shopping district.

"*Yo!*" she yelled. "Cross the street."

My mission—to find some good bookstores—was a total bust. Instead, I was able to meet back up with my tourmates, who were on the same side of town on a mission of their own.

I found them milling around on a busy corner, blending in more than you would think possible for a pastel-clad rock band. The bodyguards, too, were decked out in pajamas even sillier than the ones Mike and Tre had worn on the plane. The Buddhist monks at the temple they'd visited had made everyone buy them, so as not to disrespect the memory of Buddha with the sight of arms and legs.

In my wet Hulk suit I was the odd man out again. But I was just in time, it turned out, for another boat trip, this one a touristy cruise down Bangkok's more picturesque waterways.

For the photographers, this was another opportunity to capture some "local color." The band was put into a gondola; their bodyguards gathered at the bow like figureheads. The managers, photographers, and tailor boarded a second boat, and I took a spot on the railing at the back.

So accustomed was I to doing things on my own terms, I'd worried I would be unable to do them any other way. Now I felt like a hanger-on; that was an odd yet not unpleasant sensation. It was a luxury to follow someone else's plan for a change. "Do it yourself" was a fine credo, but not if it meant doing everything alone.

The whole scene reminded me of Al, Green Day's first drummer. He was the one who'd asked me to be their roadie back in 1990, never suspecting my tenure with the band would last longer than his.

He was the missing piece of this whole equation. He was a perfect example of the "road not taken," as well as some other roads I hoped to avoid. He was why my life had become linked with Green Day in the first place, and for that reason he was a good starting point to try to figure out how and why everything had changed. To understand the odd world I was now in, I needed to remember where we'd come from and who we'd been.

I thought of Al because of the boat we were riding in. Before touring, boating had been my and Al's main form of bonding. Every week he took me out in his canoe, usually to places where we'd get shot at or stopped by the Coast Guard. Places, nevertheless, of great beauty and an odd tranquility.

Wherever soldiers patrolled the docks, me and Al were underneath, keeping low in the boat and holding our breath—something very hard to do when slimy stalactites are breaking across your face. Then we'd row out to the open water and talk about girls for hours at a stretch.

Sundays with Al. It was a nice tradition—and a good practice run, it turned out, for what came later on tour.

I wondered if he still had that canoe. Of course he did—he never threw anything away. Not even the pile of letters, unopened, to his first band. Thinking of him, I was caught off guard by a wave of something close to resentment.

Al had always been mercilessly judgmental of other people's behavior, but he didn't stand up well to scrutiny himself. Looking back, I could see myself in him, which made me less sympathetic. We were of a similar type.

I wondered what he would think if he could see me now.

Would he be disappointed?

"You're still hanging out with those guys?" That's what he said the last time the subject came up.

Sitting on the boat, I wrote him a letter.

"Dear Al," it said.

"Me and your old bandmates are cruising down some canals in Thailand in a couple of old boats. It's pretty fun, I think you would enjoy it.

"Believe it or not, I'm on tour with them again. They lead a really weird life these days, but there's actually a lot to be said for it. They go new places every day. That keeps things interesting, always having something new to discuss. I don't love all the places or the people we meet, but I do love their determination. Remember how listless they used to be? Now they can't stop working. I love the fact that they're always facing new challenges, and facing them *together*. To me, that's success. That's something we were never against. Or was it?

"Remember when you and I started drifting apart—you and I and many of our close friends? Now we only see each other once every five years, always at a depressing party where everyone looks bad and talks about their jobs. We used to talk about fanzines and bands. With these guys, I still do. Those *are* our jobs, for better or worse, though I think we were against that, too: mixing creativity and money. That makes sense, in theory. Yet their job ended up opening up their world and provided a way for me to be part of it. Your job didn't.

"Yeah, I'm still hanging out with 'those guys.' They call me whenever they come to town. There were years when we weren't on speaking terms, but lately we talk a lot. When your life keeps changing, there are more opportunities to call, and more opportunities for reconciliation—you don't have to wait until someone dies. There's nothing like time together to get everyone back on the same page. Now I can't figure out an excuse to call you, and the last thing you invited me to was your wedding, seventeen years ago. For what it's worth, sorry I was a lousy best man. I was too young. We both were. Your mom drove us to the wedding.

"When was the last time we were on a boat together, or you were on a boat with a pack of your old friends? It's almost enough to make you think that these guys are onto something, Al. I know you've done everything you can to distance yourself from Green Day, not even cashing the royalty checks for the album you played on. I'm not sure if that's noble or stupid, but I get it. You don't want to be a part of it at all.

"But what about all our old friends who didn't pursue their dreams, who didn't fight for success on their own terms? Who calcified, who rotted on the vine? To me, that's even more sickening—yet no one's disappointed or angry at *them* for compromising. They fizzled out, they stopped producing. Our friendships were much easier to maintain when there were new albums or new issues to share, successes to celebrate, frustrations to commiserate about. Tre just came back from Cuba, studying with some drummers there, and has great stories. When was the last time you or I learned a new beat?

"I'm on this trip trying to figure out the different directions that all of our lives took. I know you're happy with yours. I'm happy with mine, too. It's quiet and bookish, for the most part. That's why I'm glad to be here, shirtless and soaking up the sun and looking at the houses on stilts that we pass. It's touristy—no Sunday with Al—but still cool.

"A small raft piloted by a Thai transsexual just pulled up alongside us with the contents of an entire bodega stacked precariously on board. Remember Bill Schneider? He's Green Day's road manager now. My old job—ha! He just bought two cold beers and handed me one.

"Here's to you."

3

BILLIE SAYS that the first time we met, he was on acid. We were lying on the hood of a car outside a show. Blatz were about to play, and Billie was playing second guitar in Blatz. I was playing second drums, so you'd think we would have already met, but that was Blatz, Eggplant's band.

Billie was nervous about playing. He kept repeating his fears again and again. "If you say that one more time," I warned him, "I'm going to smash my face against this car."

"I'm nervous," he said, either because he wasn't listening or because the acid was whispering evil thoughts in his ear. The next thing he knew, I was banging my head against the hood.

That sounds likely, but I have no recollection of it.

My friendship with Billie developed later, when we were already driving cross-country on Green Day's first tour. Back then, Al was the one I knew best. He and I were already old friends.

Billie and Mike were a few years younger than us, and much newer to the scene. They wrote the songs, but it was Al's connections and his dynamism that really launched the band. Until he joined, they'd never had a steady drummer, and Eggplant was their only fan.

Al was hardworking and extremely ethical. He got the van and booked the tour. He dumpstered a silkscreen to use for making t-shirts. Without him, it's unlikely Green Day would have ever made it out of Eggplant's backyard.

From the trash, Al also pulled some stationery from the record label IRS, and typed a phony letter expressing interest in the group. It was included in Green Day's first album, along with Al's blistering, anti-major label response. A funny prank—if he had bothered to tell the rest of the band the letter was fake.

With his oversized personality and drive, Al was the unquestioned leader, and I was Al's right-hand man—or maybe he was mine. The imbalance of power was evident in the van: Al drove and I rode shotgun while the kids sat in the back, forming their own little bloc. Al talked nonstop. Billie slept a lot. Mike read the Bible his girlfriend had given him, until one night when the temptation to toss it out the window was too great for me to resist.

It wasn't until we broke down in Harrisburg that things changed. The new transmission cost five hundred bucks. Al and I had secretly set aside exactly that much from the band fund, in case of just such a disaster. Thanks to our foresight, we were saved!

Instead of being grateful, Mike and Billie were furious. They were outraged, and rightly so. We'd gone behind their back and made decisions we had no right to make.

That's how I got to be friends with Billie and Mike: through long drives and mistakes. As they became more outspoken, their distinct personalities emerged and the dynamics of the tour changed.

Al started to burn out just as the rest of the band stepped up. He'd always been a madman, a visionary, and a bit of a missionary, but he'd never had to do it all full-time. He'd kept a very private life to offset his gregarious public front. He'd stir up trouble, then beat a hasty retreat—and always had somewhere to escape.

That was what differentiated him from the rest of the band: he had two lives. He kept a second set of books; he hedged his bets. He was a fiercely uncompromising purist with a savings account and a separate track on the side that he could switch over to when the time was right.

In this, he was in no way unique; most people have a backup plan or safety net—but not Billie and Mike. Blame Al the idealist for Green Day's later signing to a major label, for he made punk idealism seem like a parlor game for people who have other options, a luxury Billie and Mike could not afford.

Every tour has someone who cracks on the last stretch. With nowhere left to hide, Al crawled up in the loft of the van and died. He lay up there for the last two weeks, and only came down when it was time to play a show or take a shit. The loudmouthed spokesperson of the band had ceased to speak. He hit a drum to answer our questions: one beat for no, two for yes. Any question that couldn't be answered with a simple yes or no, Al responded to with a stony silence.

Mike, however, was the one who returned from tour most transformed. I'd given him a badly needed fashion makeover, cutting off his long locks and sleeves, and dipping him in bleach. The transformation was amazing, the results immediate. He disappeared the next day, only to arrive at the gig *driving* a cherry red convertible with a beautiful olive-skinned girl in the front seat.

Our jaws dropped as we watched in disbelief. It was the same old Mike, goofy as ever, yet the way others saw him had changed overnight. He returned home a new man. The Christian girlfriend was, fittingly, ancient history. Mike's kept the same style ever since, with minor adjustments.

Billie came home unaffected, except for a bad case of poison oak. You can hear him screaming about it on Green Day's version of "My Generation."

Al got accepted to college and moved away. He was a good guy, but torn between two lives, or trapped between the values of his parents and those of the punk scene—like most of us, I suppose.

He never sold out, but he didn't stick it out either. Neither with punk, nor with his various projects and plans. He was good at making a proud stand, but not a lasting one. I related to Al's dreams more than to Billie and Mike's, but Al always held back; he didn't take them all the way. He kept them from happening, in fact.

We found a diner for sale one day, the perfect spot for "Al's Cool Place," the scheme he'd been ranting about for as long as I'd known him. But when it was actually within reach, he retreated.

"I could do it," he said. "It's too tempting—so let's not even talk about it."

Billie and Mike were in it for the long run. Though I disagreed with some of the choices they went on to make, I respected them. I preferred a long and compromised struggle to a quick retreat, principled or otherwise.

Green Day did one more tour with Al on drums and me as the roadie. Unfortunately, my most vivid memory of it is not a generous one. Billie, Mike, and I are on our way from Vancouver to Seattle, two hours over the border on the American side. None of us have eaten all day, and none of us have a cent of US currency. The band fund is with Al, who is riding with the opening band. Suddenly they pull up alongside us on the highway, laughing while they shove piles of food into their mouths. Then they hit the gas, and pass.

Pissed, we drive back to Seattle and dig up the pot we buried before crossing into Canada. We smoke out in the Jack-in-the-Box parking lot, hoping the drugs will appease our hunger.

Of course, they only make it worse.

4

MY READING TASTES already tend towards the ponderous and obscure, so imagine the gems on my shelves that are gathering dust: *The Political Economy of Change in Czechoslovakia*, published in 1973; *Peddlers and Princes*, the driest account imaginable of trade and barter in Indonesia in the mid-fifties. Stuff that would put even the most fanatical coffee drinker (that's me!) to sleep, I save for trips to countries where I don't know the language, where the lack of distractions and interruptions makes it possible to really focus your thoughts. In those situations even a list of ingredients in English makes for fascinating reading, and helps preserve your sanity—for without distractions you can hear the voices in your head just a little *too* clearly.

This is why, when Billie joined me in the morning at the hotel pool, he was greeted by a "brief synopsis" of the Tamil Tigers and their long struggle for an independent state, a subject that had kept me hanging on the edge of my seat half the night. He listened with interest, but it faded as it became obvious that my point was nowhere in sight. Alas, my professor dad had taught me how to lecture instead of speak.

An armchair leftist had never been as armchair as I, sitting in one of the world's most expensive hotels, poolside. What can I say? Green Day were footing the bill, and I have feet. I dove into the pool, pools still being somewhat of a novelty to me, since I don't have one in my yard—nor a yard at all, living as I do in New York. Instead, we have all-night Indian food and the subway.

When I emerged from the pool, there was Tre. He and Billie lounged around with me for a while, but couldn't seem to unwind. A nervous tension tugged at the edges of their eyes. Tonight was the first show of their Asia tour, and they looked anxious to get it underway.

That photo was one of the few that did turn out: Billie and Tre with the pre-show jitters on the hotel roof. The Bangkok skyline looms behind.

Billie was talking about his dad, who died when Billie was very young. A drummer, he'd backed up Billie for his first shows, at age five. Thirty-three years later, the child prodigy still got a touch of stage fright.

Parents were something we hardly discussed on those early tours, when we were still just kids ourselves. Nor did Billie let on back then that he was an actual *musician*. In the punk world, that was something to be ashamed of. It wasn't until much later that he showed me a copy of his first record, "Look for Love," released twelve years earlier than Green Day's *1,000 Hours*.

As for fathers, the subject came up a lot now that most of us were fathers ourselves.

"He was a teamster, you know?" said Billie. "And just before he died, the teamsters held a dinner in his honor. They gave a big speech about how the teamsters are like family. They promised to take care of his wife and kids, and make sure we were alright. Everyone in the place was in tears."

He paused, then shrugged.

"Of course, they didn't end up doing shit. But it was a really nice speech."

Billie's mom supported all six kids by herself. After three decades as a waitress, she finally got to retire when Green Day went gold. It was cause for celebration, until a few months later when she summoned Billie for a mother-and-son talk. "I'm restless," she told him. "I miss my regulars. I don't know what to do with myself."

She was sorry to disappoint Billie, but she'd decided to take her old job back—and there she's been ever since, not at the diner where Green Day played their first gig, but just a short drive down the street.

As for my own parents, they were long gone, having died early like Billie's dad. Green Day had known them, though—that was the difference between my old and new friends. Mike remembered the cataclysmic mess of my childhood home. Billie remembered my dad's sourdough bread. "I loved the smell when I walked into your house," he said.

That was his last word on the subject of parents, spoken as he and Tre headed back to their rooms to prepare for the show. My senses perked up, suddenly remembering the piquant scent myself.

I stayed in the beach chair, drying in the sun and thinking about the differences in how we were brought up. The contrasts hadn't been apparent early on. They came out later, in unexpected ways.

5

BILL SCHNEIDER had warned me that lobby calls were strict. Stragglers would be left behind and have to find their own way to the airport or venue. There were no excuses or exceptions to the rule, even for members of the band.

Bill had his tricks to make sure things ran smoothly. For instance, Mike kept a separate, secret cell phone for his wife to reach him on. Sooner or later he used it to call someone else, then had to get *another* new phone that no one knew the number of. No one but Bill, that is. He kept a list of all of Mike's secret numbers, and in a pinch, he called every single one.

It was easy to picture Mike running around cursing while six phones rang at once. The hard part would be keeping a straight face when he showed up in the hotel lobby with smoke pouring out of his ears. Mike was not one to suffer silently.

I remembered how hard it was on the early tours to herd all the cats together when it was time to leave. The Green Day I knew were not a particularly disciplined bunch. Just to be safe, I dressed fast and took the elevator down a few minutes early, only to find everybody already there waiting. It was me they were waiting for!

Someone had whipped these guys into shape, or they had whipped themselves into shape—proof that people *can* change. I'd never seen a group of people do anything without a lot of waiting around, especially on tour. This unexpected precision was refreshing; it eliminated all the usual bickering. At 2:00 on the dot we moved quickly to a fleet of waiting vans, and were off. The site of the show was miles outside the city, as stadiums tend to be.

Driving through Bangkok's business district, we passed huge monuments to the royal family on every block. The streets were filled with soldiers and cops, as well as wannabes in mix-and-match uniforms with pictures of the king attached to their mopeds with scotch tape. This, in a country whose name translates as "land of the free."

The oppressive feelings of militarism and monarchism were so prevalent that they seemed impenetrable, yet only a few months after we were there the city was taken over by rural rebels demanding, among other things, the dethroning of the king.

A hopeful sign—until the rebels were massacred by the military, the real rulers of the country.

We took a quick detour on the way to the show in order to satisfy Billie's sudden craving for a uniform. I held my tongue, waiting outside the military supply store.

At the arena, the Green Day techs were onstage

turning knobs and tuning up. They'd formed their own band, Hearing Impaired, to play soundchecks; I waited on the empty dance floor expectantly, but my high hopes were dashed. Their set turned out to be only cover songs, and the delivery was lukewarm.

I looked around, at a bit of a loss. This was the part of the tour I'd dreaded, when everyone went to do what they did best, and I was left aimless. As a former roadie, I was used to being busy at Green Day gigs. I yearned for some role to play and some way to earn my keep. Instead, I had four or five hours to kill, not counting their set, which was another three.

I didn't expect anything more than a breath of fresh air when I stepped out the stadium's back door, but it was like passing through a portal into another world.

Suddenly the glamor was gone, and the heightened sense of tension that came with it. It was as if I'd walked out of a Vegas casino onto empty and dark streets, though the outskirts of Bangkok were sunny and bright.

Two bored-looking Thai security guards sat smoking languidly in the heat. A family carried folding chairs from their car. Going to the gig, or to the beach? Otherwise, there was no one in sight.

The stadium parking lot stretched out in front of me, and beyond it—nothing at all. Fields and trees, as far as the eye could see. I felt invigorated but a little empty, as if I'd just stepped offstage or was awoken abruptly from a dream.

For the first time on the trip, I felt the shock and thrill of being in a truly foreign place. Until then, I'd been surrounded by friends, or in areas that had seen their share of tourists. Now I had no idea where I was.

Where the parking lot ended, so did the pavement. I passed under the highway we'd come in on, then took the first turn. The dirt road was rutted and flooded in places, like those I'd walked on through farmland in the American Midwest.

I felt tipsy. Nothing I like better than walking an unfamiliar street.

A few bicyclists slowly passed, one by one. But where were they coming from?

A long metal pole blocked the road at one point, cutting off access to cars, had there been any cars to stop. The further I got, the more I seemed to be escorted by guys on bikes, as well as a few on foot who appeared out of nowhere, wading out of the thick, lush foliage that grew head-level on both sides.

I was concerned but not alarmed until I spotted a huge cluster of ragged people further ahead, gathered in the middle of the road. Just in case, I decided to take a quick right and beat a path through the bush myself. When I stepped out onto a different road, a soldier on a motorcycle nearly creamed me, coming around the corner at top speed. He drove into some sort of military base tucked into the bush, in what appeared to be a burned-out squat.

What to do? Where none of your preconceptions applied, everything was a total mystery. You could compare it to what you were used to, or just throw your hands in the air and accept that you were helpless and didn't have a clue. You could either enjoy it or let it scare and worry you.

I saw a waterfront in the distance, and leading up to it a large parking lot—yet what looked from a distance like puddles on the pavement turned out to be dozens and dozens of dogs. Upon closer inspection, they were not sleeping, but dead, with thousands of maggots feasting on their flesh.

Despite the nausea, I felt a weird sense of relief. It was idiotic to wander through a waterfront wilderness littered with dead dogs, without knowing a single word of Thai—yet it was also liberating. I had worried I'd grown overly cautious in recent years. Now it was clear my fears were misplaced: I was just as foolish and headstrong as I'd ever been.

Someday my luck would run out, but if ever there was a time to push the envelope, it was now. If I were to get hurt or arrested, Green Day would be nearby to help. It was the closest to health insurance I'd ever get.

Just as I steered around one rotting dog corpse, I nearly stumbled on another one. It was the same with the security guards I encountered when I reached the other side of the parking lot. I strode with as much authority and entitlement as I could muster, aping the gait of Green Day's bodyguards. Hopefully I'd be mistaken for an off-duty member of the US military.

One by one, the rent-a-cops waved me past.

I walked right into a gated waterfront community

filled with the type of houses favored by diplomats and deposed Third World despots: low-lying and heavily fortified. Domestic servants were the only people in sight.

Finally I reached the water itself, and put my tired feet in to soak. I opened my book to its dog-eared page, and was immediately immersed.

The Tamil Tigers had just split into warring factions, some trained by the PLO, others by the PFLP.

Riveting stuff! The rest of the world receded into the periphery.

When I emerged from my reverie and returned to the stadium, the scene seemed tame in comparison, and overly controlled. The frenetic spirit of downtown Bangkok wasn't in evidence, nor the anything-goes feeling of my walk in the outback. Foolishly, I'd thought a show in Asia might be wilder than what I was accustomed to in the States—as perhaps it would have been, at a smaller, less expensive, less remote venue.

The only spark I noticed was in people's eyes: they were glowing with an eager, though muted, energy. Even the tough-as-fuck punks who mugged it up for my photos were quietly thrilled about the concert, Green Day's first in Southeast Asia in thirteen years. For many fans, this was their first chance to see the band.

The crowd, however, was not particularly young. Ten years earlier, Green Day had been playing mostly to preteens who couldn't possibly understand the subtexts of their songs. Thankfully, the band had made it through that stage of their career. Now their audiences—in the US, and apparently in Thailand, too—were truly all-ages. More so than at your average independent show.

Even if this didn't turn out to be a completely new and unique experience for me, it already fulfilled a simpler and more pressing need. I'd been to too many lackluster gigs lately, too many halfhearted readings. Too many funerals and weddings, even, that left everyone in the room unsatisfied and curiously unmoved. What I craved was a feeling of deliverance, a spirit of togetherness. Was it too much to ask for an event that everyone was genuinely excited to be at? One everyone agreed was important? One everyone wasn't secretly eager to escape from?

I watched the crowd pour into the place, slowly filling the upstairs stands and gathering in front of the stage—ten thousand people in all. Then came a crackling announcement over the PA: "Now it is time to pay our respects to our beloved king." Martial music began to play, and while I looked on aghast everyone turned the same direction and assumed reverent, almost tearful expressions. Surely, this was irony.

"Excuse me, do you speak English? Excellent. Tell me, is this for real? Does everyone *really* love the king?"

According to the guy standing next to me in the audience, a dandy in a bowler hat in the *Clockwork Orange* style, they do indeed. However, he went on to claim that there are no Thai punk bands—a crock of shit, as any reader of Luk Haas's scene reports in *MRR* knows, so his opinion was suspect. Still, the sight of nine thousand, nine hundred, and ninety-nine people taking a stand against democracy was unnerving. Talk about feeling alone in a crowd.

I'd hoped that Green Day would lead the audience in one of the rousing chants they are famous for, like the time in Canada that Billie had the audience booing Christianity and screaming "Fuck Christ!"

Billie's mother-in-law, a pastor in Minnesota, was not too happy when she heard about that one.

Everybody together: "Fuck the king! Fuck the king!"

But it was not to be. Instead of putting his foot in his mouth, Billie used his hands. He made the biggest faux pas possible almost as soon as the band stepped onto the stage.

He began a corny Southern preacher skit. "I need a witness!" he cried, pulling a young volunteer out of the front row.

Unfortunately, Billie had not read the *What You Should Know about Thailand* pamphlet we'd been given on the plane.

"Rule #1: *Never* touch a Thai's head! It is considered an offensive, shameful insult."

The eager volunteer was facing the audience, so Billie couldn't see her mortified expression when he laid his hands on her head. The whole crowd gasped and groaned. Some even turned away, but Billie was too caught up in his preacher act to catch on. He kept his hands on her head for a full two minutes, while behind him, Mike and Tre continued to play.

"And now, you shall be saved!"

Ouch!

But at least I got the unified, moving crowd experience I'd been craving.

The band never realized what had happened. I probably shouldn't have brought it up the next day, because Billie didn't take it all that well. He seemed sore at me for mentioning it.

"We just do what we do," he said. "You can't take every single thing into consideration."

True. But maybe better to say: "Whoops! Anything I shouldn't touch in Singapore?"

6

MEALS WERE PROVIDED at the shows, but otherwise we were on our own. Food from the hotel restaurants was outrageously expensive—one hundred and fifty baht for coffee in Bangkok, where chicken satay skewers cost ten baht on the street. The obvious solution was to eat out for all meals, but in the morning the outside world was too much to face.

Instead everyone woke up early, no matter what time they'd gone to sleep, and at 10:45 there was a mad dash for the hotel buffet. Every crew member, manager, bodyguard, and backup musician arrived red-eyed and sleep-deprived to wolf down as much food as they could before the 11:00 cutoff time. Mike and Tre usually came too, just for the company. Not Billie, though—he slept late.

It reminded me of the old ninety-nine-cent breakfast special at Leshko's on Avenue A. The door of every squat on the Lower East Side burst open a few minutes before 11:00, and an army of dirtbags could be seen sprinting across the park. I'd never seen punks run before, except from the cops.

Trying to find breakfast or a bathroom in an

unfamiliar city can bring anyone to tears, even in their own country. Nothing else makes you feel quite as helpless and out of place. Not only was the food free at the hotel buffets, but we could help ourselves, which made everyone feel more at home. The various groups mingled together in a way that didn't happen during the rest of the day, when their different roles put them into separate orbits, even at the shows.

Oddly enough, the only snobbish attitudes I encountered came from the crew. They seemed disdainful of anyone not doing "real men's work," including the members of the band. My attempts to bond with them as a former roadie fell flat.

Fuck 'em—I'd paid my dues, and was now enjoying my much-delayed reward: the former roadie sunset cruise. There were notable exceptions among them, like the pyrotechnics guy, who went out of his way to be kind.

I arrived in the lounge one morning and took a table by the window. The city seemed serene, as crowded, chaotic Bangkok could only be from twenty stories aboveground. Then I looked around the room and was alarmed to find myself alone except for a few businessmen. Before I had a chance to help myself to food, a waiter came and took my order.

I was worried: was breakfast not free? Did everybody already leave? It *was* our last day in Thailand—had I made a terrible mistake and missed the lobby call?

I heaved a huge sigh when Mike walked in. Seeing me there, he pulled up a seat. Everyone else had already left, he explained—everyone but the band and me. We were on a later flight.

Mike and I had always been fond of each other, but we'd never become close the way Billie and I had. I barely even knew him outside his role in the band. When I thought of Mike, it was mostly about how funny he was. His puppet shows in the van used to have us laughing so hard we'd piss our pants, especially when he'd put on Neurosis's *Sales at Zero* and make the puppets lip-sync along.

But that was long ago, so long that it may as well have been a different lifetime. This was my first chance in a decade to talk to him at length.

Right away, I could see he hadn't changed; instead, he'd gotten more the same. His features and mannerisms, exaggerated before, were even more extreme. His cheekbones jutted out, his eyes shined on me like high beams. If I hadn't already known him I would have been scared, for he appeared like a volcano ready to erupt.

Some people aren't very present. Their minds are drifting, their attention is elsewhere. What are they thinking? You can never tell.

Not so with Mike. He is *extremely* present. Like most funny people, he's also incredibly high-strung. He held court even though we were talking one-on-one.

He and Billie were like brothers—Mike being the slightly younger one. They had completely different personalities, but were fiercely protective of each other. Mike had even lived at Billie's mom's house when they were teenagers and he had nowhere else to go.

Onstage he was the quintessential bassist, the sidekick who backed up the frontman. Offstage it was the opposite: Mike was loud and Billie was quiet. Mike was a ham—a natural comic, whose impressions were devastatingly accurate—and Billie was his partner who played it straight. They were the perfect team. But what was Mike like alone?

Sitting together, I couldn't help noticing that he and I resembled each other—not just in the matching haircuts and sleeveless shirts, but in our overall edginess. Bleach was made for people like us, with heavy brows and hands that fly around like birds, knocking over the condiments when we speak. Even with the blonde hair that artificially lightens our countenances, people always think that we're angry—and perhaps they're right.

Was this how I came across, in my constant need to be one hundred percent engaged: overwrought, and a little scary?

Yes. But I could take some comfort in the fact that my intensity could never freak out Mike. With him, I had met my match.

Sitting at that table together, we probably looked like a crazy guy arguing with himself in the mirror. Actually, we were both gushing about how lucky we felt—thankful for the people we shared our lives with back home, as well as the friends we were traveling with now. We were laughing about the unlikeliness of the two of us having breakfast together in Bangkok. Who would have thought?

Some things don't need to be said, but the unsaid things are usually the best. So we said them, over breakfast. We got sentimental about the present.

Now there was just one more band member to catch up with.

7

WHEN TRE REPLACED AL, the difference was like night and day.

Tre appeared to have no morals, no scruples, and no worries about doing the right thing. The only similarity was that both were annoying and loved attention—but Tre was downright offensive. Billie and Mike had their hands full doing damage control when their new drummer announced: "There are two kinds of women—bitches and my mom."

No one should be judged by their parents, but in Tre's case, it seemed relevant. His dad was a Vietnam vet who came home from the war feeling ripped off and used; he never put his trust in anyone again or let anyone tell him what to do. All he wanted was for his family to be left alone on the remote stretch of land he'd bought high up in the hills.

Tre was gregarious and outgoing, but with the same fierce independence and stubbornness as his recalcitrant dad. He really didn't give a fuck what anyone thought of him. In fact, he liked to push people's buttons in order to get a bad reaction. That gave him the freedom to speak his mind uncensored, which was not only his worst quality, but his best.

Al's motto on tour was "Be on your best behavior." Tre's was "Be yourself." That didn't necessarily mean being unruly or ungrateful, just unapologetic. It was more honest. Tre could be annoying or embarrassing to be around, but he wasn't ever duplicitous.

To Tre, altering or editing yourself at all was being fake. That approach became the band's. It was still evident twenty years later in little things like Billie's attitude towards his onstage gaffe in Bangkok.

But Tre never thought he was right—he just knew what he wanted and how he felt. As a result, he was never self-righteous or manipulative, and never seemed to get defensive. That quality made him unique, at least for an adult. With him you sometimes felt like you were traveling with a two-year-old. Tre was definitely the baby in the band.

I only traveled with Green Day once after he joined the group, and it was entirely unplanned—a short hitch across the border that became a month-long trip through the Canadian interior after they invited me to stay along for the ride.

Green Day were at an awkward impasse at that time. The switch from Al to Tre was less significant than the sudden boost in the group's popularity. They were still doing things the same old way, though the audiences had doubled or tripled in size. They were still booking their own shows, but the small clubs were now packed almost uncomfortably tight.

Each time we screened a new batch of shirts, we sold them all right away and had to go through the whole production again. At the end of the night, I was walking around with piles of cash stuffed into my pockets, and they were full of holes.

Besides helping load the equipment and manning the merch table, me and the other roadie had to hold back the surging crowd so that they didn't knock the mic stand into Billie's face. Two roadies can only do so much against a tidal wave—especially at small halls where there isn't a stage. After every show, I was bruised and drenched in sweat.

Finally, the inevitable happened: the audience broke through our human chain and knocked one of Billie's teeth loose. In between lyrics, he spit it out. The glint of the moon on the tooth as it arced over the crowd was one of the most graceful things I've ever seen. The look on Billie's face was priceless, too; he raised one eyebrow in a "you can't win 'em all" expression, and kept playing without missing a beat.

Something needed to change, but there weren't many models for getting popular gradually or gracefully. Green Day had a choice: they could either adjust their business and booking practices to match their newfound success, or continue as they were until there was no way out but to make a quantum leap.

Their choice wasn't a conscious one, I think, just a lack of decisiveness and an inability to compromise or find middle ground. It's always easier to let things get so dysfunctional and overwhelming that you're forced to make a clean break—not just in relationships, but in every facet of life.

Tre wasn't the main reason for the restless feelings Green Day began to have, nor the previously off-limits ideas they began to entertain. Yet he tipped the scales in a direction quite different from the one I was headed in. Unfortunately, I got stuck in the role of cheerleader for the scene they were starting to outgrow. I was a handy example of the stubborn-headedness of DIY punk—an extreme to measure themselves against.

Some nights, everything I said or did seemed to make them roll their eyes. I couldn't help feeling like the girlfriend they were about to dump.

The more Green Day shirts we sold, the more they started to charge for each one. I thought we should be lowering the prices, since shirts were cheaper to buy in bulk. To them, that attitude reeked of socialism or middle-class guilt.

"There's nothing wrong with making money," they patronizingly explained.

On one all-night drive, I offered everyone sandwiches.

"We made a thousand dollars at the show," Mike laughed, "and you're still making peanut butter sandwiches!"

Then he helped himself to one.

I was glad to share my food, but it bothered me to be so completely misunderstood. I would have preferred a nice steak dinner. Unfortunately, Green Day didn't pay me, and peanut butter was all I could afford.

That had never been a problem before. Every tour I'd been on had either broken even or been a loss. Now that money was coming in, it complicated things.

It wasn't a lack of generosity on the band's part, for they'd always been incredibly generous. Up until then they'd never been able to regularly feed or pay themselves. Paying me would've added a weird dynamic to our friendship—but unfortunately so did *not* paying me.

That was an unwelcome side effect of success. They were at an awkward crossroads in their career, and I was in an awkward position somewhere between roadie and guest.

I felt bitter. Sad, too, to see our lives moving in different directions, and feel helpless to alter their course.

That was a turning point. There was no fight, no official goodbye, but I never asked to travel with them again, and they never asked me.

The time had come for us to part ways. I felt at home in the underground, and Green Day were headed on to bigger things. Their way of touring had already become too businesslike and routine for my tastes. I missed the days when we traveled by the seats of our pants, Billie driving and me riding shotgun while we listened to the same Ramones tape over and over. When he got sleepy, we found a mattress factory and crashed out on the discards by the dumpster out back.

Now it was a new era with Tre on board, and I was old baggage—not quite Al, but cut from the same cloth. They didn't need an older brother looking over their shoulders and telling them they were wrong, and I didn't need anyone low-rating the values I'd staked my life on.

Right at the end of the tour, I turned twenty-four. Returning from a stoic, solo birthday dinner at a diner, I walked into a truly unexpected surprise party at the house where we were staying, complete with candles and a cake that Green Day had baked.

Yes, they had always gone the extra mile for me, even though we didn't always see eye to eye.

In the years that followed, I roadied for many other bands: Unwound, Chino Horde, Dillinger Four, Wardance Orange, I Farm, and the Fleshies, among others. I liked the excitement of new bands on their first time out, with cancelled shows and vans broken down on the side of the road.

But rarely did I feel the same fraternal bond I'd had with Billie, Mike, Al, and Tre—and rarely did the other bands' music move me the same way.

What I missed most was the talk. Other bands turned up the tape deck to drown each other out. With Green Day, touring was one long conversation, mostly about women: women's bodies, their ways, their attributes. We had long and uninhibited discussions, mostly about sex. I'd heard of women opening up to each other like that, but never men.

I'd assumed that male "locker room talk" would be derogatory, but with the Green Day guys, that was not the case. Mike's rapturous and loving descriptions of giving head forever changed not just the way I talked about sex, but the way I thought about it. Their frankness cast off my veil of fear and shame. Everyone spoke about his own actions and instincts without shyness, and enumerated the details of lovemaking as if talking about fine art or fine cuisine. There was nothing demeaning about it. Even Tre's cutting comments (in Thailand: "I think her tits were smaller than mine") seemed harsh only because they were the plain truth.

I'd always been a romantic, but all too often I used that to camouflage the fact that I was uptight. Sex was a subject I alluded to but never actually discussed, as if to do so was shameful or base. As a result, I'd been in the dark my whole damn life. Comparing notes with Green Day helped me realize that my fears and fantasies weren't necessarily unique. That was a revelation, and totally freeing.

The funny thing is, sex itself was never a big factor or a common occurrence on those early tours, even after Tre joined the band. It was mostly just talk. Certainly it wasn't a major focus for us the way it is for others on the road. On the first Green Day tour, Billie didn't get together with anyone at all. Women outside the Bay Area weren't into him back then.

I had one make-out session on the muddy banks of the Mississippi, but the woman who struck me most was further north. I was crushed out on her immediately, but she was not interested—not in me, at least. She was the exception to the rule as far as Billie was concerned.

I didn't even see him speak to her, but he got her

address somehow, and began a courtship through the mail. Four years later they were married. Soon their eldest son will be taller than me.

If Billie ever felt weird about me saying that his wife was hot, he's never mentioned it. In my defense, anyone who isn't charmed by Adrienne when they meet her is a total moron.

As it happens, I was also there, on a different tour, when Bill Schneider got together with *his* wife.

Even the roadies get lucky from time to time. I met my present girlfriend when she and I were roadies for different bands on tour at the same time.

So much for promiscuity on the road. It all ends up so damn wholesome—unless, of course, you're Tre.

But the person who was the most secretive and moralistic on the early Green Day tours turned out to have been the biggest slut of all. And we never even saw him kiss anyone.

8

I WAS EXCITED because I had a long-anticipated mission: a search for a series of books published in Singapore in the seventies. The bindings were bad, the print runs were small, and the titles were fated to remain obscure. The selection was a mixed bag, but the *Writers in Asia* series had turned me on to many authors I would never otherwise have found, a few of whom were absolutely amazing. The series was almost impossible to find—and I only had half of them.

Once in a blue moon, someone from Singapore wrote to order a *Cometbus*, and I begged them to find me the titles I was missing. The response was always the same: "They are out of print, and Singapore has no used bookstores."

I hoped to prove them wrong. Even if they were right, there had to be somewhere where old books could be found, no matter how far off the beaten path. Books rarely get thrown away, even when they deserve to be. They have a life of their own.

My hobby, in recent years, has been tracking them down. I collect foreign novels and obscure histories for the same reason I collected stamps and coins as a kid: they make my tiny, troubled world seem a little less claustrophobic. They give me a feeling that the world is a large and wondrous place. Searching them out has led me interesting places, if not necessarily to the particular volumes I hoped to find.

Though they say it can't be done, I've learned more about life from books than from experience, because from books I've learned from *many* people's experiences and seen the world through many people's eyes. They've taught me not just history, but empathy. I've even learned more about sex from books than I have in bed, though I have a lot more reading to do.

I knew a little bit about Singapore, too.

Perhaps my knowledge of the world was dilettantish, but it was better than none. *Son of Singapore* by Tan Kok Seng taught me about Singapore in the fifties. *Man of Malaysia*, his coming-of-age sequel, clued me in to the interconnectedness of the two countries, which were once one. Neither book was great, but they gave me a basic understanding of the region on which to build.

From there, I read on. Children's books, anthropological studies, labor histories—they all told variations of the same story: a tiny country, extremely wealthy compared to its neighbors, whose secession—like that of most small, breakaway nations—was encouraged by outside forces eager for greater access to its resources. Imagine New York City declaring independence, and you'll get the picture. Overnight, Singapore went from an old-fashioned trading post to a world banking capital. Now it's the world's busiest port.

Every Singaporean novel I've found is about change. "So is every novel," you might say, and you'd be right, but for Singapore the change came on like a hurricane. The move towards modernization was a blind rush that left many people emotionally and literally displaced. The overnight shift made changes in the Lower East Side or San Francisco seem minor in comparison.

All this I knew, yet I still wasn't prepared for what I saw when I got off the plane, which was—gasp—LA!

Echh. The whole thing looked like a fucking mall, or yet another airport, neither of which have used bookstores in them. Perhaps my pen pals were right.

Our first stop was a lavish dinner of the best local food, courtesy of the local promoter. In every country on the tour, we had a similar feast—a tradition of hospitality particular to Asia, I believe. That was another part of the routine which wasn't hard to get used to. The disconcerting thing was that these Asian Bill Grahams—and most were white—were my age. So were the high-powered Warner Brothers aides who occasionally made appearances backstage. However, that was all we had in common. They were not the type to trifle with used books.

Luckily, the promoter had a young assistant who was of great help.

We sat in a circle at a huge table piled high with baked crabs, surrounded by disturbingly colonial-themed decor, as tastefully nostalgic as a plantation in the American South. Amidst cracking and sucking noises, the assistant put me on the right track for my search.

The annual library sale was Singapore's best place to score books, she said. Naturally, it had just passed. Local used bookstores were scarce but not nonexistent. She drew up a map.

Now I was eagerly anticipating the hunt, but my mind was at ease. I could put my obsession aside until morning.

The dinner itself was festive and remarkably sweet, the prevailing mood of the tour so far. Green Day all sat together again, and not for the benefit of the photographers this time. Everyone made jokes and comments that showed they knew each other better than they knew themselves—or at least their memories were less selective when it came to other people's mistakes.

"I've never gotten anyone pregnant by accident," one band member boasted. "Me? No. Thank god. That's *one* thing I've never done."

"Sure about that?" I asked, giving him the eye.

"Oh, right," he said. "Never mind."

Later we all sat together in the hotel lobby drinking beer. The late-night talk, once about women, was now about children. Oddly enough, it was much the same: everyone shyly bragging and showing photos, worried about being far away and what the future would bring.

Tre and Mike's eldest daughters were just hitting puberty, which terrified them to no end. Billie worried about his sons' bad grades and their final exams coming up later that week. Like any traditional working-class parent, he wanted his kids to get the education he didn't, and grow up smarter than him. For Billie, the whole "American Idiot" thing wasn't just shtick—he was hard on himself for his perceived shortcomings almost as much as he was defensive about them.

The only problem was, he set a terrible example. It was precisely Billie's lack of education that led him to pursue a career in music, and that pursuit brought him riches and fame. How could he convince his kids of the importance of good grades? And how did I find myself once again explaining to a dad that a report card isn't everything?

At the fancy—but public—school Billie's kids attend, they get called freaks. Everywhere else they go, they have to deal with Billie's fame. It's a miracle they'd turned out so well-balanced and cool despite it all.

Getting to know them had been one of the best parts of my rapprochement with Green Day. Any weird feelings about your friends becoming parents are quickly forgotten when their kids get old enough to start a pit. Billie's eldest son and his friends had saved my night at a recent show where the rest of the audience was too uptight to move or show any emotion at all. Their enthusiasm was refreshing and contagious.

"Seeing you dancing with them blew my mind," Billie said in Singapore. "They're the same age I was when we first met."

He was getting sentimental now, as he usually did when drunk. He kept following me outside the hotel to talk. Tre pulled me aside: "Don't take Billie for a walk."

Already the old roadie thing was happening, each person whispering in my ear about the other guy, but on this tour it wasn't to complain, but to gently advise.

"Tre's stories aren't always *exactly* true," one person whispers. Another warns: "When Bill Schneider says *everything is totally taken care of*, it means something is either cancelled, on fire, or about to explode."

Billie gets wide-eyed and mischievous when he drinks, gung-ho about any bad idea that's brought up. It's gotten him into plenty of trouble in the past, though he usually slips away at the last minute before setting out on whatever mission he's embraced.

"Hold on, I have to piss," he'll say. Soon, he's curled up asleep like a baby, usually in the bed you already claimed and made. That happened countless times on our old tours. You've never seen someone so victimized and misunderstood as Billie when you tell him to move his ass and go find his own place to sleep.

Mike excused himself: "I'm going to go read my book and pass out, something I do more and more in my old age."

I should have asked him what book it was.

Last call was called, but a few of us were still at the bar nursing the dregs of our drinks. Slumped in lounge chairs nearby, the bodyguards were half-asleep, each keeping one watchful eye on his sheep. Billie was telling a story about being in the steam room of a hotel in Hollywood.

"Suddenly I hear footsteps, and out of the mist

steps this creepy old guy, and he's buck naked. 'Okay,' I'm thinking, 'this is kind of awkward.'

"He's got long hair, thinning a little on top. And he's just standing there, looking at me.

"He starts making conversation. 'Is it hot enough in here for you? Do you want me to *turn up the heat?*'

"I'm like, 'Oh no, this is getting really weird and lame.'

"Then he asks me, 'Hey, are you in a band?'

"Oh god. So I say, 'Yeah, I am.'

"'So am I,' he says.

"And that's when I realize: 'Oh shit! It's *Roger Daltrey*!'"

9

I'VE EXPLAINED how Billie met Adrienne, his wife. But Adrienne isn't the only person we met back then who forever changed our lives and the life of Green Day.

On the first tour, a kid approached us and gave us a demo of his band. That was Jason White. Like all punks from Little Rock, he soon moved to the East Bay. Jason and I shared a room; before long, we shared an ex-girlfriend, too. Jason's band, Chino Horde, took me on tour, the first of many in my post–Green Day roadie career.

Through me, he got to know Billie. They were enamored with each other right away.

"Hey guys, want to walk around?"

"Walk around? Hmm. What do you think, Jason?"

"I don't know, Billie, it might be more fun just to stay here playing acoustic guitar with you all day."

"That's what I was thinking, too. Enjoy your walk, Aaron."

Hmph. It was annoying, but not the first time I'd introduced two people and wound up as the third wheel—nor the last, I'm sure.

Had Mike and Tre not nixed the idea, Green Day

probably would've become a four-piece right away. Slowly but surely, Jason started playing with them anyway, beefing up the sound for a few TV specials and live acoustic sets. Though he never became an official member of the band, Jason has been with them ever since, appearing not on records or in promo photos, but onstage at every show.

Other people might chafe at the second-string role, but not Jason; he likes to be part of the picture, but a little off to the side. A co-pilot type, he leads with his style rather than his ego. He isn't worried about getting his way. He's Southern, meaning neither ready-to-fight nor overly polite, just genuinely easygoing and eager to avoid conflict.

For a long time, Jason was on his own in the shadows of the stage. Then he was joined by another Jason: Jason Freese, a jack-of-all-trades. Freese plays keyboards, saxophone, accordion, and whatever else is necessary. Jeff Matika is the most recent addition to the group. An old Arkansas friend of Jason White's, Matika plays guitar. This tour of Asia was his first with the band.

White, Freese, and Matika. Together, they make up the Big Three.

When I first heard the phrase I assumed it meant Billie, Mike, and Tre. Instead, the Big Three is the self-deprecatory title that the unseen, unheralded musicians have given themselves, poking fun at the fact that when they arrive at the airport or emerge from the limo, throngs of Green Day fans look disappointed and stare past them hoping to spot someone *actually* in the band. Only the most terrifying Green Day groupie would recognize any of the Big Three after they'd stepped offstage.

Anonymity has its benefits: the Big Three can walk around unbothered. But being an integral part of the performance every night without much acknowledgement must be difficult. They are employees, in an odd limbo between being band members and part of the crew. Neither Freese nor Matika is as entrenched as Jason White, who also happens to be Billie's best friend. What makes it especially hard for Freese and Matika is the fact that both men have newborn babies at home. They spend a lot of time on the phone.

Back when Jason White lived in Little Rock, pool hopping was the local punk pastime. When I visited him there, we got busted at every single one. With that in mind, I gave his room a ring when I woke up in Singapore. Down below was an Olympic-sized swimming pool with no one in it. For better or worse, we didn't have to hop the fence to get in.

Across the sky-blue water and under the clear blue sky, Jason and I drifted like a pair of icebergs. Our paleness was glaring. I'd left New York in the middle of the worst winter in years—with few regrets—to go on this tour. As for Jason, he's just not the outdoor type, except maybe at night. Mid-January, and here it was eighty-five degrees in the shade. Neon yellow birds flew by. They hurt our eyes.

Jason clearly enjoys the music as well as the

companionship of playing with Green Day, yet if it were all to end tomorrow, he would probably be fine—maybe even relieved. He and his wife could move back to the Mississippi Delta, where she'd taught in a literacy program for poor kids. Jason's old bandmates would be a short drive away. They'd never stopped playing together, though their music had shifted from Dischord-inspired hardcore to roots rock 'n' roll.

Of all the people in Green Day's inner circle, Jason seems to have the most to fall back on. Because of that, I could ply him with questions that would be too insensitive, if not outright insulting, to ask the rest of the band. The most pressing of them was, "Where do you go from here?"

While everyone else was either celebrating Green Day's success or sniping about it, I worried for them. Popularity is hard on people. So is obscurity and failure—yet nothing could be worse than breathtaking success followed by a swift fall from grace. No one wants to be a has-been. But where else can you go from the top but down? When the inevitable happens, how will you handle it?

That's what I wanted to know: what's the escape plan?

They'd been through it once before, in the late nineties, lean years for the band. The audiences had gotten progressively smaller and record sales had dropped off. The albums I liked best were relative failures for reasons that had nothing to do with the quality of the material. Many factors were involved, like timing, artwork, and marketing. All of these—plus the direction the wind happened to be blowing that day—contributed to low sales for the brilliant *Insomniac* and *Nimrod*—just as they had contributed to the earlier record-breaking sales for *Dookie*. The whole thing was a total crapshoot.

Their dramatic "comeback" with *American Idiot* in 2004 caught everyone unaware. They'd managed to stay on top ever since. But for how long—and how would they weather the inevitable fall from grace when it came?

Jason surprised me with his answer. "I'm looking forward to it," he said, while making it clear that he wasn't in any particular hurry for that eventuality to arrive. The massive audiences and five-star hotels were, for him, a fun novelty rather than the norm.

Until then, I hadn't realized that this tour was unusual; the shows were bigger and the hotels fancier than even Green Day were accustomed to. "I can't even buy food at the hotels where we're staying," Jason lamented. "I have to go out and look for something I can afford."

A dog-eared Lonely Planet guidebook lay by his beach chair. I took a quick peek at the map before toweling off and heading out myself.

Out on the streets, Singapore was as different from Bangkok as could be. There was no garbage, no vendors, no blind beggars. No careening mopeds, jerry-rigged tuk-tuks, or military jeeps tried to run you over every time you stepped off a curb. At major intersections, you couldn't even cross the street; pedestrians were forced to take an escalator down into an underground mall, from which it was difficult to escape.

I managed to locate a used bookstore tucked into a corner of an old shopping center. The clerk there knew the series I was searching for, but had only a single volume in stock—one of the few I already owned. She directed me towards the other side of town and wished me luck.

Singapore looked a little like Battery Park City, pleasant but sterile in an upwardly mobile way. Posted signs reminded people to lock up their bikes: "Low crime does not mean *no* crime," they warned.

Happy couples flew kites. Fake-old footbridges arched along the waterfront. I found a quiet walking path and followed it between the buildings and highways. Unnaturally healthy-looking people passed by in the other direction, interrupting my thoughts.

When I came to the Arab district, I was disappointed. It was more like an Arab theme park than a genuine neighborhood. Little India had a bustling bazaar, but it, too, was heavily geared toward tourists.

Among the crowd, I spotted a familiar face: Bill Schneider! Standing next to him were Billie and Tre, mere dwarves in comparison. Both waved their arms to attract my attention.

When I approached, Bill shoved a fleshy yellow thing in my face. "Here, try this," he said. "But don't smell it. The local delicacy. It smells like shit."

Indeed it did, and the taste was nearly as bad. Well-versed in the ways of Bill, I chose a pea-sized piece. Tre ate the rest and was soon off in an alley recycling his lunch.

While it was fun to travel with Green Day, it was a real treat to just run into them on the street—to casually cross paths and agree to meet back up in a few hours, like we used to do in Berkeley. After a little slapping of palms, I continued on my way.

Micah Chong, Green Day's bass tech, had given me the lowdown on Chinatown, the next neighborhood on my list. Micah is Hapa Haole (half Chinese and half Japanese, from Hawaii) and had learned about local race relations from a half Chinese promoter he'd befriended.

Chinese are the African Americans of Singapore, Micah told me, though they're actually the ethnic majority. Chinatown is the old ghetto, encroached upon on all sides by modern development, and shrinking at a steady pace. The area represents all that Singapore once was and would now like to forget.

When I arrived, I could see the problem: the buildings were antiquated and showed signs of wear. So did the residents. People were working with their hands and using the curbs as a seat. There were no malls, and no other tourists in sight. Not only did I feel at home, but I found what I couldn't have hoped for in my wildest dreams: an entire six-story building full of used bookstores.

My search had paid off in spades. On the top floor,

a bookseller named S. Jawahar Ali smiled knowingly when I mentioned the Heinemann *Writers in Asia* series. He led me to a full shelf.

English is one of Singapore's national languages, but that means little; it is spoken differently everywhere, and not by everyone even where it is official. Up until that point, I'd solved the language problem by avoiding any kind of transaction. I'd avoided public transportation and any situation that might make me feel dumb and out of place.

All that was well and good, but emerging from the Bras Basah complex, I realized I was late.

Nothing like necessity to make you throw caution to the wind. I chased after every bus and asked for help not just from the drivers, but from everyone aboard—help with directions, the currency, and the best route to our hotel. It felt good to have to break out of my shell. Once engaged, Singaporeans were more down-to-earth than they had at first seemed. With the assistance of many strangers, I ran up to the hotel just in time to jump into a van heading to the show.

The auditorium was teeming with life when we pulled up. Forklifts were moving heavy equipment and crews were rigging up the last of the lights. Winded from my run, I took it easy, wandering through the maze of hallways, admiring all the hidden action that concertgoers never get to witness. Behind the scenes, it was a whole different experience, as industrious as Oakland's produce district late at night, or one of the Soviet socialist realist novels I like, with everyone working together on a massive project that no one will ever know they played a part in helping create.

Caterers were setting up a banquet-sized feast in one room; a fleet of security guards was being briefed in the next. Following the signs and flashing my pass at every turn, I came to the various offices set up for the band and crew: one for the managers, one for the *tour* managers, one for the photographers, one for the pyrotechnics, one for the opening band, one for the tailor and wardrobe and first aid. A gym, a practice room, a family room, a VIP room—all set up exactly the same at every venue, with the same framed posters of the Rolling Stones, the Beatles, and the Ramones. At the very end was the dressing room for Green Day.

Inside, Billie was stretching. Jason White adjusted his jacket in the mirror. The Plimsouls played on the portable turntable. Mike jumped rope to get his heart rate up, in order to avoid having a heart attack when they ran out onstage.

Down the hall in the practice room, Tre was warming up on drums. A distant roar told me that the opening band was over. That was my signal to leave.

I waded into the audience, looking for pockets where the crowd was most tightly packed and the people seemed the most wild and free. I wanted to get naked and do the worm—to really cut loose. What else was the point of being far from home? Unfortunately, I was white and a head taller than the average Asian. Losing myself in the crowd was not an option.

I followed the eyes of the audience, who all seemed

to be staring at the same thing. Soon I came to a crew of people who stood out even more than me.

A tight knot of eight or nine guys were gathered in front of the stage with their arms around one another. A few women were with them, but not drawing the crowd's attention, since the women were not seven feet tall, with orange turbans and long, flowing beards, like all of the men. Their faces were defiant and beaming with pride. "Sure, we stick out," their expressions said, "but we don't give a fuck because we belong here just as much as any of you."

That was the expression and attitude I'd been trying to muster up my whole life, so I went over and joined them, hoping it would rub off.

The streets of Singapore may have lacked the gritty spirit of Bangkok, but the Singapore show was everything the Bangkok show was not. In Bangkok, the band had seemed out of touch with the audience. Ballads had been thrown in just as the momentum was beginning to build, and Billie urged the crowd to dance to the least danceable numbers.

In Singapore, Green Day seemed ready. They were in tune with each other and the audience, and played as if someone had turned up the flames under their feet.

From the opening chords of "21st Century Breakdown" to the acoustic finale of "When September Ends," the Beards were jumping up and down and screaming the words, and so was I. It felt great to sing at the top of my lungs. I'd forgotten how cathartic it could be, and how wonderful it feels when your own off-key voice blends with thousands of others to make a beautiful harmony—especially when the thousands of people are quite different from you.

Every security guard in the place stared at the swarthy, turban-wearing troupe beside me, and the Beards defiantly stared back, laughing and hooting and hugging each other. Then the tense moment came that everyone had been expecting: the tallest of the group reached into his backpack. Slowly, something shiny emerged with his hand, and the whole crowd around us drew back.

Then he unfurled it: a Malaysian flag! As I'd suspected, the Beards were neighbors from the poorer, predominantly Muslim country across the water. As the Beards held their flag aloft and pogoed, the rest of the crowd booed, yet it was in a playful, not unfriendly way. Then the tallest Beard folded up the flag, and with a mighty arm, hurled it onstage.

That was my cue. All-access pass in hand, I tore through the audience and leapt over the barricades. I ran to the stage and grabbed the flag before one of the security guards could throw it away.

It hangs on my office door as I write these words. A blazing sun surrounded by stripes, reminding me of the Beards and their jubilant, defiant, contagious pride.

10

TRE AND MIKE, like Billie, had grown up in difficult circumstances. That wasn't something they talked about much—not until Green Day were accused of selling out. Even then it was journalists, not the band, who raised the subject. They framed Green Day's success as a rags-to-riches story, dismissing the band's critics as spoiled, sheltered brats who'd never known what it was like to live in need.

That description was somewhat apt, but it also applied to the vast majority of Green Day's fans. Anyway, it was beside the point. Green Day weren't just some poor kids who'd pulled themselves up by their bootstraps—they'd been helped along by a whole network of people working without pay. A lack of profit motive was part of what made the punk scene unique; Green Day would never have gotten to tour or put out records had they had taken the traditional path in the first place. Pitting the band against their "purists" critics was a convenient way to avoid any real discussion about major labels or any real dialogue about class differences.

It was the same old shit: the great American myth.

Green Day's decision to sign to Warner Brothers was made to seem like a foregone conclusion, and anyone who questioned it was either a zealot or a fool. The mainstream media had a field day treating DIY values as either a pipedream or a complete joke.

Of course, that was salt in the wounds for the punks, adding to their feelings of having been used.

Tre and Mike were better equipped than Billie to face the backlash. Mike had never been all that invested in the punk scene, and Tre just didn't give a fuck—or at least that's what he liked people to believe.

Billie was vulnerable because he really did care what people thought. He was one of the most thin-skinned people I'd ever met, completely ill-suited for fame and the pressures that came with it. One bad review affected him more than a stadium full of screaming fans. One childhood pal protesting outside a Green Day show (Eggplant, reportedly, though he denies it) was enough to break his heart.

Billie never got over the feeling of being ostracized. The more persecuted he felt, the more paranoid he got. He started taking any criticism as a personal attack.

Green Day drew inward. They closed ranks and became a family—a family like Tre's, with an "us against the world" mentality. If they hadn't had enemies, they would've had to invent some, for acting defensively made it easier to squelch any doubts they may have had themselves.

They surrounded themselves with people who

were unswervingly loyal and unconditionally supportive—people who hadn't deserted them in times of trouble. But with no one around to point out their faults and mistakes, they became cut off and isolated from the rest of the world.

Unfortunately, the same thing happened to all of us—to me, Al, Eggplant, and the whole punk scene we'd been part of. Everyone split up into little self-serving sects. Like the New Left, we split and split again. Green Day actually managed to maintain a larger circle of close friends than most of us did.

My friendship with them survived their rise to fame, but ran aground when my own life changed in dramatic ways, mostly having to do with the deaths of my parents. I was too young then to know how to deal with grief, and so were most of my friends. As a result, I lost a lot of them.

I had other things on my mind at the time besides the problems caused by punk going mainstream, but those issues were like a high-tension wire that ran through our lives. They affected everything, and exacerbated our already existing differences.

For instance, my friendship with Al turned sour when he called me up the day after my mom died, laughing about the death of Kurt Cobain. My friendship with Billie went bad after my dad died and he didn't call at all.

Billie's fame made it difficult for me to reach out to him. There were so many people bugging him for support of one kind or another, and I didn't want to join the line. I closed up, as I tend to in a crisis. The letter I later wrote expressing my frustrations, he took—predictably—as an attack. We didn't speak to each other for years after that.

I mention all this not to elicit pity or to dish out blame, but to explain another factor in the story of why Green Day and I parted ways. The choices they made had side effects that were not obvious at first, or as simple as the difference between independent and major labels.

Change is a part of life. So is death. Yet it's almost impossible to emerge from either with all your friendships and relationships intact. That's part of the pain of growing up.

11

A FEW YEARS AGO, I wrote that I'd quit my job as Green Day apologist, a thankless position and hopeless as well.

Imagine yourself as Billie for a moment, happily reading a *Cometbus* on the porch while the kids are off at school and the wife is knitting on the couch. Just when the story is getting good, there's a joke thrown in out of left field, and it's at your expense. A personal dig, and totally superfluous—at least that's how it seems.

Billie was proud of his band and didn't feel apologetic for anything they'd done. What the hell did *I* feel like I needed to apologize for?

The answer was complicated. I'd been trying to figure it out for years myself.

Every time their name came up, I also felt proud—yet I felt defensive too, for what followed was often an insult or a joke.

I always took the band's side against their detractors. They were like family to me. Who has a perfect family or isn't sometimes embarrassed by the things they do or say? But if anyone else insults them, you rise to their defense—even if you happen to agree.

I remained a fan. I wore out every new record and followed their career from afar. I felt the same way about Green Day as I did about Berkeley: both had changed, yet I still loved them deeply, and they remained a part of me.

But always having to defend the band, I never got a chance to express or even acknowledge my own frustrations with them.

My friend Rachel had the same problem; the small fishing village she grew up in had also changed. Why bother trying to convince anyone that the *Hamptons* were ever cool? Even for her, it was hard to believe. The only people that liked the place now were people Rachel couldn't stand. She couldn't even say where she was from without receiving an earful of opinions of one kind or another, and having to deal with other people's mistaken assumptions about how she grew up.

No one would ever see the Hamptons through her eyes, or see Berkeley or Green Day through mine. Neither of us could go home again. Why defend places we couldn't afford to live, or a band whose shows we couldn't afford to attend?

Finally we both gave up. She kept the fishing village in her heart, and I did the same thing with my time in Berkeley and my tours with Green Day. They were like the boyfriend Rachel finally dumped. After years of struggling to see his best qualities, we could laugh together about all the ways he sucked. We could admit his faults as readily as we admitted our own.

Let's just hope they don't get back together next week!

Which is what happened, I suppose, with Green Day and me. No sooner had I given up trying to make excuses for them, we ended up back in bed. As often happens, it was my declaration of independence that brought us together again.

You see, Green Day had always been supportive of me. They'd never said an unkind word, which is why my offhand comment hurt.

I heard Billie was upset. And so, I broke the ice. I called him and apologized. That was part of the rapprochement that led, step by step, to him asking me along on this Asia trip.

Years had gone by, and I'd come to realize that having friends was better than being right—or feeling wronged, and endlessly holding a grudge. Now I could see how I'd let my grief isolate me and cut me off from many of the people I cared about most—people who had passed out of my life but could never be replaced.

In retrospect, I wished that I'd given my friends the benefit of the doubt, and been better at reaching out. That was why my reconciliation with Green Day was so meaningful, emotional, and sweet.

Touring again with them was, to a small extent, a second chance to get it right. Now I was making up not just with Billie, but other estranged old friends like Jason White and Bill Schneider.

As for the tensions that came between us in the first place, all I can say is that some fights you're still angry about in the morning, others you're not. Some differences you work through, some you work around, and some you just accept or ignore.

The tensions and differences between us would probably always exist, but they kept our friendships electrically charged when they weren't tearing them apart.

There was something else: backstage at these concerts was a group of people who'd known me almost as long as I'd known my own parents. To say that they were like family was no exaggeration.

12

"OH, TO BE LOVED," said Jeff Matika as we walked past throngs of rabid fans at the Singapore airport waiting for a chance glimpse of their idols. Of all the handmade signs held aloft, none said "We love the Big Three."

"Be patient," counseled Jason White, "it only took ten years for me." Jason nodded in acknowledgement to the occasional diehard Green Day devotee who yelled his name.

Everyone draped themselves over chairs in the airport lounge. The conversation was about the big break-in during the show the night before, news of which had just arrived. Enterprising thieves had tunneled through two rows of hedges and a metal fence, then sawed a hole in the wall of the shed where the merchandise money was kept. Thirty grand was their take! That's a lot of T-shirts.

So as not to put my foot in my mouth, I kept silent, waiting to see the general response. The merchandise rights were contracted out to companies who produced and sold the stuff, then gave the band a cut. Mike and Tre's laughter made it clear that the band wasn't the one who took the loss when something went wrong. In fact, they were boasting about the caper as if they had pulled it off themselves.

"I'm gonna open a bar," said Tre. "Come on in! I'm rich as fuck! Gonna buy a hut. I'm going back to Malaysia where thirty grand will last. No more working at the T-shirt stand."

Mike said that, as a former thief, he had respect for the people who'd pulled it off. Had it been his own business that was burglarized, he would surely have felt differently—though wouldn't we all? I remembered the time Green Day left their entire band fund on the sidewalk outside a club in Chicago. They were complaining about that "theft" for years.

Admittedly, a daringly executed caper was easier to romanticize. Billie and I had completely deflowered the local country club once, filling his car with posies and pansies for a ballet dancer he was trying to court.

"Whatever happened to her?" I wondered. "I guess it didn't work out. Some girls don't like flowers—or grand gestures."

Now Billie's bandmates were members of the very same country club, out on the course playing golf with NOFX. Looking back was bittersweet.

On the plane, everyone was playing "Aging Rock Band," an ongoing joke about the toll that years of touring and recording had taken on their health. Tre had just had his third knee operation. Billie was worried about losing his voice.

"It's a long flight today," he said.

"Thanks," replied Jason. "I had the material tailored to fit."

The punch lines were always non-sequiturs—that was the joke; after two decades of shows, no one's hearing was intact. Still, the band was in great shape, better than almost anyone I knew. Playing music was the best workout possible. Just running back and forth on those huge stages added up to a few miles a day.

Of all the odd questions I was asked when I got home, "Do Green Day have their own private jet?" was the most common. The answer is no. They do have a whole fleet of motorcycles, a mobile pirate radio station, and a tattoo gun—but those toys don't come along on the overseas tours, unfortunately. The jets we traveled on weren't Green Day-owned, but the first-class provisions offered a semblance of privacy, with seats that folded down into coffin-like compartments that were separated from each other on all sides.

There were other amenities as well. Stewardesses cruised the aisles passing out little travel packs with all the necessities you might need or were likely to have lost. Between the flights and hotels, I had a lifetime supply of toothbrushes at the end of two weeks.

Before leaving on the tour, all I knew was that we were going to go to China. I had my fingers crossed for the rest of the itinerary, hoping for Indonesia, Malaysia, Laos, Cambodia, and Vietnam. When I received the tour schedule, I couldn't help feeling a little disappointed. It read like a State Department list of US investment and military deployment: Thailand, Singapore, South Korea, and Japan—foreign countries, yes, but squarely in the US sphere of influence. All four are permanently occupied by American troops!

Now we flew over Vietnam, which had long ago taken care of that problem. It was the only Asian country where I knew enough of the language to buy stamps and complain about cops. I pressed my face against the window. Likely as not, it was as close a view as I would ever get.

China was the reason I'd chosen this tour instead of the other options Billie had offered: South America or the South Pacific. The bad news had come after we were already on our way: the Beijing and Shanghai shows had both been cancelled.

Now we were going to Hong Kong instead. Technically it was part of China, though its status as a British colony had ended only a dozen years earlier. Touching down there, I had low expectations and a sour feeling that I was touring with the USO.

Luckily, my feelings turned out to be unfounded.

By now I was used to the drill. It was exhilarating to be part of a well-oiled machine. We walked briskly through the airport, almost at a run. We passed through a line of waiting fans, then were bundled into a fleet of idling, unmarked vans. This time, though, we were driven only two blocks. Moored at an old dock by the airport was an ancient sailing ship.

A salty old skipper helped us aboard, then pulled up the gangplank and drew the ship away from the shore. Along the waterfront the billboards of Hong Kong blinked on and off, drenching us in red and white. I felt like a spy, or a character out of a Graham Greene novel.

In the galley dinner was served, but the crashing of the waves had made me queasy. Water lapped on the ship's hull, serenading my stomach and calling its contents to come out. Soon the waters of Hong Kong harbor and ten cups of airplane coffee would flow together. Like birds in the sky, they recognized no borders—wild and free.

"It's steadier down below."

That was Tre, poking his head out of the hold. Famous for being a pig, his nurturing nature was lesser known, yet just as prevalent. He also happened to be an excellent cook.

"Are you sure?" I asked, readying myself to puke. "Wait, do you have a boat?"

"Two," he replied.

He was right about the turbulence. But *two* boats? That was over the top.

On one side of the river was Hong Kong, and on the other, the motherland itself, mainland China, home to a fifth of the world and still such a mystery. Seventy years ago it was feudalistic, non-industrialized, a virtual colony. Now it has other troubles, but is at least in charge of its own destiny.

For me, it had always been symbolic. Besides its own fascinating history, China represented the limits of my own ambitions and possibilities. Long ago I'd come to the realization that you can't do everything, or everyone, in one life. You have to pick and choose.

For example, Billie chose fame. Now he can't walk down a city street anywhere in the world without being recognized. I made choices based on my own options, and ended up with a frugal life spent mostly around books, desks, and cats. We're both pleased, I think, with how things turned out, yet still aware of what we've given up.

China was the example I always gave. "I'll never make it to China," I said. "But that's okay. I can read about it instead."

The fact that Billie could offer me a trip to China but I couldn't offer him anonymity showed the imbalance of our situations and perhaps in our friendship as well. I had provided him a bridge to places and scenes he wouldn't otherwise have seen, but not to the extent that he had for me.

Perhaps it was fitting that I now stood like Moses, gazing longingly at the Promised Land but unable to get in. Lucky guy, he died before he could see what became of his kids. They crossed the border and slaughtered the Amalekites, then the Hittites, then the Canaanites ... right up to the modern day.

Israel, bah! There was a lot to be said for wishing for something and not getting it.

On the roof of the boat, Billie, Mike, and Tre were mugging it up for the pesky English photographers, running through some halfhearted poses. "Now one for me," I said, when the limeys had packed it up.

My photo caught Green Day looking quite different from the way they appear on the covers of records and magazines. They are dancing around playfully, enjoying each other's company, neither foolish nor faux tough. Too bad what I got back from Walgreen's was just three blurry figures with red eyes.

After a long day of traveling in boats, vans, and planes, I was beat. I retired to my hotel room as soon as we got ashore, but the phone rang just as I was starting to read. It was Billie, asking if I wanted to join them at the hotel lounge. That, too, was part of the routine, one I usually took part in, though bars were something I traditionally shunned.

Every day, we made elaborate plans to go out on the town at night, but by the time we arrived at the hotel everyone was exhausted and overwhelmed, yet still too restless to sleep. Instead of going out, we met up in the hotel lobby for a drink.

It was a way of being in public without having to leave our safety zone. There were never more than a handful of other patrons, just enough to mix it up with, without being bothered too much. For Green Day it was like drinking on the porch.

In Hong Kong, however, the hotel bar was different. It was crowded, loud, and gaudily opulent. On a tiny stage, some once-legendary jazz musicians played. A young couple was seated near us on an awful date. The guy kept trying to kiss the woman he was with, too clueless to realize she wasn't interested. A middle-aged drunk made the rounds, telling his life story. The tuxedoed waiter scraped and bowed. Despite his obsequious act, he obviously despised and felt superior to everyone in the place.

"This is hell," I thought. "We are doomed to play every one of these roles ourselves. Right now we're on top of the world, but this is what's in store."

It was terribly depressing, especially after one of the bodyguards hit it off with the middle-aged drunk. They sat arm in arm reminiscing about their military service—and security work they'd done for contractors in Iraq.

Could I have misheard him? Suddenly I felt sick. I wanted to wash my hands. I stepped outside the hotel to catch my breath.

Not for the first time, the differences I had with Green Day seemed not minor but like the difference between life and death. One moment I'd be filled with tender fondness, then all of a sudden this visceral reaction that made me want to crawl out of my skin. It was a warning sign.

Some things are like that—they strike you as repugnant for instinctive reasons, probably having to do with your culture and the way you were raised. The French word "gauche" comes to mind, but I preferred the Yiddish word "treyf." Literally, it means not kosher, but I also use it to describe things like cars, bars, strip clubs, guns, dogs, rock 'n' roll, and football games. Things that are treyf you avoid, not because you hate them per se, but because in avoiding them you keep yourself from becoming like the people you hate.

For instance, Orthodox Jews don't hate pigs, they just avoid eating them—a totally arbitrary rule but one which is there for a reason. Start eating pork and soon you'll be sleeping with your neighbor's wife.

I suppose it's unnecessary to say that the same is true for punk. The whole elaborate system is set up to keep people in check. Break one small rule and you start down a slippery slope, which is where I sometimes felt I was with Green Day. They had become part of popular culture, impossible to separate completely from all the things that made me sick. I couldn't shake the feeling that somewhere in the basement of Abu Ghraib was a little radio playing "Basket Case."

There were times that I'd had to draw the line, and Green Day were on the other side. That was hard to reconcile, because they were my friends.

Was Green Day treyf?

I was drunk, much drunker than I thought. I decided to clear my head by taking a walk. I'd only had one beer, but famous lightweight that I am, that was more than enough.

I stepped out into central Hong Kong staggering a bit and was surprised to find it humming with life—humming like a sweet song you sing to yourself. A feeling of enchantment passed over me. Every city has its particular spirit, or lack of it, but I hadn't expected to find one so captivating here. It was the perfect antidote for my caustic mood.

Here old and new were beautifully juxtaposed; neither one seemed to be winning the fight. In between skyscrapers were ramshackle stands—still open long after midnight—selling handmade rubber stamps. The city was hilly, with crooked, terraced streets criss-crossed by alleys and crumbling stone stairways that I stumbled up.

This was an old habit of mine: the revenge walk. I took them less to explore than to set myself apart—to grab life by the horns whenever lethargy and complacency seemed in danger of setting in. These spiteful journeys were meant to prove something, though I wasn't quite sure what, other than the quickest way to get lost.

Oh, how I wished I'd drank some coffee or had the foresight to borrow a bit of the local currency before impulsively stepping out. Some joker had put a 7-Eleven on every corner to mock me, even on the smallest deserted streets. I peered through the windows, ogling the metal urns, undressing them with my eyes. There was coffee inside, but I had not a cent to my name, only some leftover baht from Bangkok.

Even the presence of 7-Elevens amidst ancient buildings seemed playful rather than jarring. Hong Kong was the exception—the woman you love for breaking all your rules.

Double-decker busses drove by, and even cooler double-decker cable cars. I set up my own scenery, a courtroom in which to try Green Day—but try as I might, I couldn't find a charge that would stick. Even on the relatively minor infraction of not wanting to join me on this late-night walk, I found them innocent.

They'd played for three straight hours the night before, then had a four-hour flight. Tomorrow they would do it all over again. It was amazing that they endured that kind of grind year after year. *I* hadn't even wanted to go on a walk, but had forced myself out of spite.

If it came down to a court case, there were plenty of other people to try. How about the old flame of mine who was now interrogating prisoners in Afghanistan? Guilty, beyond belief. The first girl I ever kissed, now a jailer? That was a harder call. Jailers—like judges, such as myself—could also be sympathetic, or even social justice advocates, supposedly.

My old traveling companion would probably claim the same thing. Lucky guy, he'd just gotten a voucher for a free dinner when I saw him last. The restaurant Mike owns gave them to *every* cop on the Oakland police force.

Where had we all gone wrong?

I came to a park. It was quite late, but a few people were still out, mostly young women strolling alone or sitting on benches reading books. One stood on a street corner carrying on a conversation with herself. She had her arms crossed in a theatrical way, as if practicing for a play. She rolled her eyes and tapped her toes like someone tired of being kept waiting—yet neither her impatience nor her entreaties seemed to have any effect.

When I got closer, I spotted her audience: a frolicking, frisky cat, who rolled around on its back and rubbed itself against her feet, having found its own perfect time and place to take a break.

13

I AWOKE REFRESHED, and opted for a walk—a peaceful, not spiteful one—rather than join the crowd at the hotel buffet.

Remarkably, the city's mystique had not diminished with the passing of the night.

For a lover of alleys and winding staircases, Hong Kong was paradise. In their grandeur, the old stone stairways reminded me of my native stomping grounds. Though I try not to compare other places to where I grew up, even the temperate climate was strikingly Berkeley-like; so was the way a deceptively short climb led you right to the crest of the city's highest peaks.

The presence of public bathrooms made me think that Hong Kong was the more humane of the two places—until I scaled the last stretch to the top and found gated luxury condos blocking my way.

I stomped and cursed. Then I spotted an open fence and got very quiet. Quickly, I slipped inside.

It was some sort of water treatment plant. Huge sweaty pipes led off into the distance, reaching all the way around the ridge. I used them as a walkway, ignoring the warning—or welcome—signs.

Further on, the pipes went underground and were replaced by storm drains and a narrow access path. Butterflies frolicked around miniature waterfalls made by the floodgates.

"This is working out rather well," I thought.

Man-sized palm fronds tickled my sides as I walked. Huge brown hawks flew overhead. At other stretches, the forest grew over me like a canopy, blocking out the sun and sky so that all I could see were shades of green. Frail, pale, paper-thin leaves crackled under my feet. I gathered a few to show to a botanist friend back home, but when I did she chided me: "Those aren't leaves, you idiot—they're snake skins."

I slipped into fantasy. The first, predictably, was about sex. A woman approached me on the path. She stopped me with a silly excuse and then began to laugh. What was the harm in it? Like a tree falling in the forest, no one would ever know.

But no sooner had she dressed and continued on her way, I realized I had made a terrible mistake. Even a tree falling secretly and anonymously can have a disastrous effect. It touches off a landslide, a forest fire. The last known specimen of an endangered species is killed in the blaze: your honesty; your chances for happiness.

I felt guilty. I switched tracks.

Walking the other way through the deep, green bamboo were the Ramones! With them, I was safe. But they were upset; Tommy had just quit. "No problem!" I told them, "I play drums, too. I even have a Ramones name: Casey. What do you think?"

No good. The Ramones were dead. The Buzzcocks came next, skipping through the bush. Not the Vibrators, but the Buzzcocks. *That* was one mistake I'd never make again, as I had in an interview, discussing records I'd played for Billie. So I'd mixed up two '77 penis-related UK punk bands—was that really so unforgivable?

I had to admit, though: there was a big difference. The Vibrators I wouldn't even recognize walking through the forest. I'd probably passed them a thousand times.

The reality was almost as unlikely as my dreams: in a crowded city of seven million, I'd been walking for hours without encountering another human being. I was getting a little loopy as a result. The storm drains were lined with oversized metal wheels that I stood at playing "captain of the ship." The rusted levers looked like medieval torture devices, but my enemies, damn them, were on a different continent.

I'd almost forgotten where I was when the forest came to a sudden clearing and the curtains of foliage parted to reveal a sweeping view of the city below. It was dazzling but also dizzying, for I could see that I'd been walking for miles along the edge of a cliff.

There was a small, plush patch of shrubbery, most likely some variety of poison oak. I lay down in it so as to better appreciate the panoramic view.

Hong Kong was stunning, stretched out before me—from the harbor all the way up to the fancy condos at the top of the hill, which I was now inexplicably above. Their posterior was like a massive wall of television sets, each window showing a different scene.

Unfortunately, it was all humdrum stuff: not one couple going at it on the rug, much less a murder in progress. I chewed on a hotel apple in lieu of popcorn.

I felt a little embarrassed. If anyone were to see me there, I'd look just like a cartoonish caricature of my younger self—an image I'd done everything in my power to shake off: the overgrown boy, dreamy and nostalgic, with no money and no map, sitting on a hillside taking notes. The fact that I was once again traveling with Green Day didn't help.

And yet I couldn't have been happier. I'd never forgotten these simple pleasures, but it had been a long time since I'd wholeheartedly embraced them. I was surprised to find that my old clothes still fit. I felt rejuvenated, as if recovering from a long illness or just getting out of jail.

Billie had conveyed the same feeling in our brief conversation at the hotel bar the night before. Performing for new fans, and going places where they'd never been—like Singapore and Hong Kong—made the old songs feel new again. It was a reminder of why they had formed the band in the first place, and served as a much-needed shot in the arm.

I looked out over the cliff. If only I could leap over the obstacles in my way: the condos, the churches, the fancy hillside homes. Further below I could see the dregs of the city teeming with life—the tenements, the outdoor markets, the crowded streets. I had only one full day in Hong Kong and I wanted to experience more than just trees. I returned to the path, but trees were all I got for another hour, without even a clearing to gauge how far I'd come. I was antsy for the path to end, especially as the sunlight began to wane.

Without warning, four workers came along in the other direction wearing soiled undershirts and safety helmets. They nodded and disappeared into the undergrowth like ghosts, leaving me alone. When a woman with a beagle came next, I felt confident that the trailhead was close. Indeed it was; the path disappeared as quickly and completely as the workers had, and I found myself on a residential, almost suburban street. A family unloading groceries eyed me uneasily as I emerged from their backyard.

I began my descent. Soon I was back in that wonderful only-in-Hong Kong mix that anywhere else in the world would have been a total mess.

Space-age commuter trains ran up the side of the hill, discharging passengers on remote stony outcroppings. Schoolchildren chased each other along adjacent footpaths. Old women tended garden plots and cheerfully strolled up terrifyingly steep and ancient stairways. There were cars, too, winding above and below on Escher-like roads.

At a trolley stop, I was finally able to check a map. Somehow, after all that wandering, I wasn't far off course. If I cut through Hong Kong Park I'd be right on the mark, and not a minute too soon, for night was approaching fast.

Still, I couldn't resist a peek into the park's aviary when I passed. At the pay toilets in Bangkok, turnstile hopping had been turned into a fine art. I successfully employed the contortionist tricks that I'd watched.

Blame the dream-like quality of being alone in unfamiliar surroundings for the fact that my mind was drifting wildly. One minute I was watching the birds, the next I was writing imaginary newspaper headlines.

"FORMER ROADIE IN CUSTODY" read one.

"Cometbus, an illegal alien who listed his occupation as 'former roadie,' was taken into custody yesterday after disrobing and climbing into a tree with a yellow-beaked Saskatoon ..."

"MYSTERIOUS HERO!" That was better.

"A disheveled-looking blond man saved the lives of Xbo, Ffdx, and Br, three schoolchildren on a field trip to the Hong Kong aviary, when a trolley ran off its tracks, crashed through the fence, and came to an abrupt halt after connecting with the stranger's abnormally large feet."

As for the birds, they were brilliantly colorful, but no more stunning than the hawks I'd spied from my mountain perch.

I was running now, late for the show. Never mind the opening band, it was the caterers I was worried about missing. They would start clearing away the food when Green Day got onstage, and I hadn't eaten anything but an apple all day.

14

THERE IS BUT ONE more person to mention from the first Green Day tour, and I promise he will be the last. He, too, played a huge role in my life over the past twenty years, though we went in separate directions after that tour and I've never seen him again. We didn't share a room or play together in a band, and he didn't marry one of my close friends. The last I heard of him was a postcard from Provo, Utah, in 1991. Yet I've thought of him often in the years since.

His name was Geoff, and he played bass in a mediocre band that glommed on to some of Green Day's shows, as mediocre bands are wont to do. Soft-spoken as he was, I never would have known his special qualities had I not noticed him gone one night. The next day I asked where he'd been.

It turned out that he, like me, went out to explore each city after the show. But while I returned late to wherever it was that we were staying, Geoff simply found a doorway, put his wallet down his pants, and went to sleep. In all sorts of weather and in all sorts of neighborhoods, he threw caution to the wind.

When he told me this and saw my surprised response, he shrugged: "What's there to be afraid of?"

He was a bit of a drunk, which no doubt helped, since it's harder to pass out in doorways when caffeine is your drug of choice. Still, Geoff had guts. He went out into the heart of the city and into the heart of the night and made himself at home. Bright and early he'd wake up or be woken up, then find his way back to the van in time to get to the next gig.

He wasn't an idiot, or one of the many people I've met who purposely put themselves in danger as some kind of self-inflicted punishment. He wasn't crazy or blindly confident. Strange to say of someone who chooses to sleep outside on concrete when a soft bed is available, but he had common sense. His sense of personal freedom just happened to be stronger than his sense of propriety.

He was the real deal. Compared to Geoff, I was a half-ass hobo on a milk run. I ran from home but kept one foot on the base. He upped the ante by casually doing what I hadn't even imagined possible. His example was the green light I didn't know I'd been waiting for.

In the following years, I carried his memory like a talisman, using it to give me the courage to take chances, especially when there was no other choice. I slept in bushes, under bridges, in boarded-up buildings and in storage sheds. One particularly dismal night, I camped in a graveyard outside a tiny village in France.

Dogs howled at me from just outside the cemetery gates. The wind whistled through the tombstones, extinguishing my candle. I was cold, scared, and in a country where I couldn't speak enough of the language to explain myself if caught. I thought of Geoff, who wouldn't even think twice, just tuck his wallet into his pants and shut his eyes. And so, I did the same. What was there to be afraid of?

His influence came at the same time as my parents' illnesses. Seeing them bedridden or in the hospital brought out an unexpected response: it filled me with a terrific rage to live. It was a constant reminder that life is short and shouldn't be put off. When they died, that was one less thing to be scared of. I tried to live two, three times as hard.

The only problem, and not unrelated, was that I couldn't sleep. Even in a warm bed, I had trouble surrendering to dreams. It was hopeless with any air conditioning or even the slightest breeze. Only once, on the roof of an abandoned school in Greece, was I able to lay down outside and immediately pass out—and that wasn't for long. A family of Gypsies found me there and brought me home.

I had learned a lot from Geoff about taking risks. Outside and on my own, I did feel more free. Too bad I couldn't learn from him how to sleep.

When I thought of that first Green Day tour, I thought of Geoff, Jason, Adrienne—all the great people we had met along the way. But the shows, with few exceptions, were nothing to get nostalgic about. The "crowds" were small and hopelessly shy. In Pensacola, I had to pick up the sitting members of the audience and carry them to the front of the stage, only to have them immediately abandon their chairs and run away. They lined up against the back wall as if Green Day were a firing squad. Who could have known that they really did have something to be afraid of?

But that's how most of the shows were on that first tour: awkward and not particularly exciting. The huge concerts Green Day played now were actually a hell of a lot more fun. The only thing that hadn't improved was the opening act. In Hong Kong, I watched them play from backstage while I busily laid waste to what was left of the deli trays.

I couldn't help comparing the current clowns to Geoff. The thought of these guys sleeping outside was hilarious. Their velvet pants would get soiled, the locks of their chemically straightened hair would be tragically blown out of place. Did they even *own* shirts, or just the white leather jackets they took off after the first song? The only place I could imagine them going out to was a bar.

Geoff's band hadn't thrilled me, but they'd had a certain little something, and their own particular style at least. *These* guys were a third-rate Hanoi Rocks, at best. Green Day knew how to pick 'em. When it came to opening acts, they had a weakness for insipid, unoriginal glam.

"Alright, Hong Kong!"

They were broaching Spinal Tap territory now. It

was obvious they had done a lot of practicing, most of it in front of a mirror. They took insincerity to a whole new level, or were so sincere about making it—in the music business and with the ladies—that nothing else mattered. They did seem genuinely thrilled to be living the rock 'n' roll dream, something I happen to despise.

Too bad, because they were such nice guys. Predictably, I hit it off best with their older roadie, himself a former member of a similarly styled old LA band that was actually great. If only the tables were turned and he had been the one onstage! But roadies think that about every group.

After one or two unwarranted encores, they blew kisses to the audience and haughtily cast aside their beer bottles after draining them in one gulp—beer bottles filled with water, which the roadie dutifully collected and refilled to use again at the next gig.

A man in a bunny suit came out next. He did a dumb dance—the same every night—to warm up the audience in between bands. Behind the mask was a "secret" member of Green Day's crew, who'd been my next-door neighbor in 1989, and whose loose change, lost between cushions of his couch, had kept me alive for weeks at a time.

Back then, he was ridiculously uptight. Now he danced around like a moron in front of millions. I marveled at the transformation, but the results were embarrassing. The bunny routine was the kind of tribute to drunken stupidity you would expect at a frat house or a football game. Besides, it was disingenuous:

even the beer bottles the bunny guzzled were water-filled props.

The Village People's "YMCA" finished, and a different tune came over the PA: the Ramones' "Rock 'n' Roll Radio." That was what we'd all been waiting for—the cue that Green Day were about to come out onstage. I wedged my way into the crowd.

Green Day were the ones with all the theatrics, the light show, and the pyrotechnics, yet compared to the warm-up acts, Green Day were Chomsky! They were a beacon of straightforward sincerity. They weren't afraid to lay the schmaltz on a little thick at times, or get all the hands in the house up in the air for an extended sing-along. Still, their showmanship was a breath of fresh air after what had come earlier because at least it was genuine.

Not only was the audience more impassioned than on the old tours, but so was the band. Even if the 1990 version of Green Day were playing next door, I wouldn't have budged from my spot near the stage, except for the fifteen-minute "Shout" cover medley toward the end of the set. I liked their old songs about girls, but the depression and confusion of their later material had more bite. Maybe it was all the same thing: rejection and a feeling of being disenfranchised—but now it was more anxious and to the point.

I wondered about the psychological divide between the audience and stage, which punk had been hell-bent on destroying. Experiencing it on this tour for the first time, I found that I rather enjoyed it. Green

Day's inaccessibility allowed the audience to focus on something outside of themselves. It gave them a chance to step out of their skins and forget, for a few hours, their own problems.

In a massive crowd, that was easier to do. Just being part of a huge audience was a moving, almost spiritual experience. I'd never known that before, having almost exclusively attended small, independent shows.

I was like a kid who'd never been allowed to watch TV or eat sugar cereals. Arena rock was something new and fascinating to me, and I was lapping it up. Once the novelty wore off and I felt sick, I'd go back to the books and whole grains on which I was raised.

It helped that there were none of the annoying aspects of an American concert here—no drunk yahoos or people you saw in the halls at high school. A big concert was a good way to bypass the isolation that came from being in a foreign country. Everyone was pressed up intimately close, and the ear-splitting volume made conversation impossible. Instead, we used our bodies and our eyes to speak, and our common language: the lyrics of Green Day.

I remembered something sweet but confounding that Billie once told me: "There are two people I want to impress when I write lyrics—you and Bono."

I still wasn't sure how to respond to that one, except to sing along.

Bono?

The audience here was, of course, different from

one at home. In a white, suburban audience, I would have been busily looking for things to set me apart from the crowd. Here, it was the opposite: I could enjoy sticking out.

Were these people conservative? Rich? Mainstream?

No clue. All I could tell was that they were Chinese.

My appearance was what set me apart, not my beliefs. That was a refreshing change.

When the lights came on, I was surprised to find the opening band standing nearby. I reassessed my low opinion of them. Any band that was also fans was alright by me.

Later it became clear that they hadn't been mingling without a purpose: the dressing room was filled with women they'd presented with special backstage laminates. The shirtless singer pointed out the one he liked best, sending the roadie over to play fetch. The singer was just a kid, and the woman he picked didn't seem all that into him, but she accepted her clichéd role half in jest. Soon they were making out.

I sat in a corner with Billie, Bill Schneider, and the Big Three, literally turning our backs on the whole thing. Then I felt something cold and slimy slip down my shirt. I turned and let out an involuntary scream: it was Tre, with a *live octopus*, one of whose tentacles was reaching into my pants!

It was truly a nightmare. Tre cackled evilly as he pulled the octopus off me. Then he opened his mouth wide and began to devour it alive! He had mentioned a desire to try some of the more unusual local delicacies, but I hadn't taken the part about live animals literally.

Tre had taken one bite before the octopus wrapped one of its tentacles around his neck and started to squeeze—first tentatively, then with more force. The octopus got another tentacle down his throat, and Tre started to choke. All the while, the limeys were in a frenzy of flashbulbs, egging him on.

Billie and I turned away, too revolted and unsettled to watch—only to see the opening band's singer sucking the girl's face and slipping his hand underneath her skirt. It was all too much.

The bodyguards did not step in to save Tre from the octopus, but once he'd freed himself from its grip, one went with Tre to the bathroom to help him puke. The other two hacked away at the still-writhing animal with knives.

Get the singer for the opening band, too!

Where Tre had gotten a live octopus, I never did find out. I was scared to ask.

Later, he joined us at our table. He seemed sobered by his near-death experience, and looked a little pale.

"I ate everything as a kid," he said. "I was the only kid you didn't have to convince to try something new.

"Last week, Mike's wife asked me how she could get their son to be like that. He *hates* vegetables.

"I told her to get a job driving big rigs cross-country. That's what my parents did. They left me and my sister alone for weeks at a time. You learn to cook pretty fast that way. You eat anything you can find."

15

I WAS IN AN unreasonably good mood on the flight to Korea, smiling at all the wreckage around me.

"You like to see us looking rough," Tre observed.

It was true. I lived for moments like these, when everyone was at their worst. Not since New York's last heat wave had I seen so many people lose their humanity overnight.

I surveyed the scene, licking my lips. This misery was the essence of tour, and until now I hadn't tasted it. Everything else, as the rabbis say, is commentary. Everything else is window dressing. Everything else is just a distraction that keeps you from getting to the grit, the pith, and the pain. And that's the whole point! Tour, like life, only begins when you finally break down on the side of the road and have to ask for help.

Okay, so Green Day had some monstrously exaggerated form of Triple A—but that didn't save them from breaking down themselves, as the title of their most recent album suggests. Everyone from the band members to the bodyguards was a broken-looking mess. Our whole wing of the plane was hungover, sleepless, and completely and utterly worn out. We looked like we'd gotten the shit beaten out of us, or had mind-blowing sex—right before getting dumped.

Everyone looked strung out. They looked awful in a beautiful, sensual, vulnerable way. Everyone but Tre, who looked absolutely great, a picture of good health and good cheer. Dressed in a handsome peacoat, he strolled the aisles making conversation with the stewardesses, not in a lecherous way but like a hyperactive, overcurious kid. I'd never seen him in such good spirits.

That was Tre: he thrived on chaos; he ate evil for breakfast. He purposely crashed the car then leapt out of the wreckage unscathed. He hummed a happy tune while the other passengers limped out barely alive from the smoke and flames.

This time, the crash had been Tre's post-octopus eating urge to find a tank of live piranhas. Apparently the octopus had merely whetted his appetite—either that, or he wanted to give the animal kingdom a chance to bite back.

Only a select few were interested in joining Tre on his search, one that was likely to stop at every sex club in Hong Kong en route. Choosing moderation and decency, the rest of us decided to retire to the hotel bar instead. That, however, was our mistake: measuring moderation and decency in relation to Tre. We ended up drinking ourselves right over the edge, thinking all the while that we were playing it safe.

Those who'd followed Tre had, of course, fared even worse. Why search for piranhas when your tour guide himself is a man-eating beast?

The night had ended with one of the photographers getting dipped headfirst into a tank of live sharks—not once, but twice.

Any guess as to who was holding him upside down by the legs?

That was a picture I would have loved to see—but, like all of the best moments of the tour, it went unrecorded. So did the pink-streaked sky as the sun rose over Hong Kong Harbor. I was marveling at it from my window just as Tre's search party returned to the hotel. I could hear the limey photographer cursing Tre in the hall. "Fuck off!" he screamed. "I'm an adult. I don't need a fucking wake-up call!"

And so, when the limey failed to show up a few hours later in the lobby, we left without him. He managed to somehow make it to the airport on his own, but with only minutes to spare before our flight.

I looked at him now, sitting across the aisle. So this was an adult—the thing I'd heard so much about. His face was beet red, and a stream of drool trickled down his neck. Gingerly, I removed the camera from his bag, just to give him a souvenir of what life looked like from the other side of the lens.

Click!

At moments like this, I wished I was the one doing the Green Day coffee table book, not the two limeys. While they were asleep or with Tre watching women shoot ping-pong balls out of their orifices, they were missing all the best stuff. It was tender moments like these that I wanted to frame: the ghoulish, unshaven army all muttering to themselves in their sleep, and Billie, snoring, passed out facedown across a whole row of seats.

What a great cover shot that would make!

Hovering above it all was Tre, smiling like a proud dad. He was a weird dude, and kind of dark. Yet he was honest with himself. Whether or not he liked himself, I wasn't sure, but I related to his self-deprecating humor better than, say, Mike's occasional self-righteousness. Billie had neither of those qualities; he appeared to be led along even though he was the one calling most of the shots. It was these subtle dynamics and interactions between them that I longed to capture. That was what made them a band.

In the past few days, everyone had been getting fed up with Tre's antics. The photographers were gasoline for his fire, goading him on toward ever more outlandish acts. Eating live animals made for lively photographs, as did whoring it up in the all-night sex clubs, but his bandmates and managers found the whole thing annoying and immature.

What need was he trying so hard to fulfill?

And then came the answer: *the same need all of us have*.

But the way he went about it seemed kind of desperate and sad.

The fact that Tre was single and everyone else was married and settled down didn't help. Tre's behavior was something they had outgrown—or so they told themselves, not without a touch of remorse. It couldn't be easy being on tour with someone who'd slept with more women in a week than they had in years. That was bound to bring up weird feelings. At least, it did for me.

Tre and I had always had a competitive vibe between us, a guy thing. We'd never been interested in the same women, much less intimate with them, as far as I knew. Despite that, Tre seemed to see me as a threat. When he had a girlfriend, he didn't introduce us, and I was careful to keep my distance. I had that same irrational fear about a lot of my friends: the fear of someone taking my place. Sex is where our insecurities come out the strongest, but sex probably didn't have anything to do with it. That kind of rivalry was a chemical, or animal, reaction—maybe even a fucked-up form of mutual respect.

Maybe it had to do with my friendship with Billie.

There was something else, interesting though probably irrelevant: Before Tre was in the band, I'd actually played in Green Day. Oddly enough, I'd forgotten all about it until I'd pictured Billie raking leaves.

Why was I waiting for them to rehearse in the living room? It had taken me a full minute to remember: I'd been rehearsing *with* Billie and Mike at the time.

We only played a handful of shows together. I was filling in for Al at the time, for reasons I cannot now recall, possibly having to do with his old girlfriend. She was extremely volatile.

Besides the shows we practiced for, there were at least two occasions where I was called in to pick up the sticks at the last minute. At one, Al had to rush off to stop his girlfriend from drowning herself in a nearby lake (it turned out to be only five feet deep). The same thing happened in Pennsylvania on tour, while he talked her off the ledge over the phone.

I was the suicide-watch substitute, and though I added my own unique style to the songs, I was no match for Al's sureness. When it came to Tre, I wasn't even in the same league.

Twenty years had passed since then, and Tre had improved in leaps and bounds, while I was still playing the same beat—a fierce one, mind you, but not particularly malleable. Perhaps it felt weird to have another drummer looking over his shoulder while he played. I hope Tre knew that when I did, it was in awe.

In hindsight, I wondered if Al had been grooming me to be his replacement in the band. It was fun to imagine what might have been—but *that* list went on and on. Playing drums in Green Day was but one of a million lives I might have had. I could also have stayed with the Gypsies in Greece, or been devoured by dogs in the French graveyard.

When we landed in Seoul, everyone stepped off the plane as if in shock. In Thailand, we'd been led straight past customs without even getting stamped, a sign that both Thailand and fame were corrupt, with their own special set of rules off the books. In Korea, the only special treatment we received was the extra scrutiny from Passport Control.

While waiting for the line to move, I posed for

pictures and signed scraps of paper, not bothering to tell the starry-eyed autograph seekers that I wasn't in the band. However, when I stepped up to the Customs window, I made that fact very clear.

"Musician?"

"No, beautician."

At our previous ports of call, I'd stated my occupation as chef, cobbler, hairdresser, and fitness trainer. Try as I might, I just couldn't answer a question the same way twice. It was an instinct that had gotten me into a lot of trouble over the years—rooted, most likely, in a family legend about the czarist army. Since only sons were exempted from military service, my great-grandfather and his brothers each spelled our family name differently on the forms, thereby avoiding the draft and sure death—for Jews were always sent to the *front* of the front.

I hadn't managed to inherit their survival instinct, only that one particular trick. As a result, I gave a different name, address, occupation, and social security number every time I was asked. When it came time to change a flight or appear in court, I had a lot of explaining to do.

It was a bad habit, but anything was better than saying you were a musician. Unless, of course, you *liked* having a gloved hand up your ass.

The drummer for Green Day's opening act learned that lesson in Seoul. Poor sod, he probably gushed proudly to the passport guy, telling him all about life on the road.

His bandmates went ahead to the hotel. They didn't even realize that their drummer had been detained until he showed up three hours later, livid and needing to borrow money for the cab.

The same thing had happened when Green Day visited the White House. While the band got the deluxe tour, one of their bodyguards was quietly led away to the torture chamber and waterboards. It was a simple case of mistaken identity—someone else with the same name on the terrorist watch list. But it remained a sore subject. Whenever anyone cracked a terrorist joke, one bodyguard did not laugh.

The temperatures had dropped as we traveled north. Hong Kong had been chilly in a Bay Area way; in Seoul it was still winter, with a foot of snow on the ground. That didn't deter the faithful coterie of female Green Day fans who were waiting outside the hotel in the cold. Dressed in heavy coats, they shifted from foot to foot as if needing to piss.

When I passed them again on my way out, they perked up in excitement for a moment before realizing that I was no one important. Then they frowned and shot nasty looks, angry at me for letting them down.

I sneered back. No wonder the crew guys were such shits: getting this sort of treatment day in and day out was hell on your ego. It made it almost impossible not to get resentful at both the fans and the band.

It was cold and late, but I was lured out by all the promising signs I'd seen on our drive from the airport to the hotel. *Coffee Story* seemed like a curious name for a business, with its byline: *Hear the tasty story of coffee and deli.* But as we drove on, there was a sign on every store: "Coffee," "Hot Coffee," "Coffee!!!"

Had Seoul gone coffee crazy? Apparently so. Even the bars included it on their marquees: "Whiskey Beer Coffee," "Beer Wine Coffee," "Coffee and Beer."

Immediately I could tell the difference between Seoul and an American city. Here the drinking spots were brightly lit, and buzzing with life rather than vomiting it up. Sitting at the window tables were whole families, packs of teenagers, and young couples on dates. All of them had coffee mugs in their hands—and it was 1:00 AM!

The neighborhoods of Seoul had the same qualities that make me head for the Asian areas of New York on Friday and Saturday nights: a sleeplessness, a lack of drunkenness, a feeling of shrouded mystery, a sense of personal safety. I'd expected Asia to be completely different than the Asian-American enclaves in the United States, but the differences seemed negligible. Hong Kong was like a thousand Chinatowns placed side by side. Seoul had fancy areas like Manhattan's K-town and residential areas more like the K-town in Queens.

I went into a few markets, curious if they resembled the Korean groceries of New York, known for their fastidiousness and immaculate sense of order.

Not so much. The Korean markets in Korea were a little looser and less rigid. Same with the Koreans themselves.

Besides the late hours I kept and my penchant for dealing in cash, I didn't have much in common with most Asians. So why, I wondered, did I feel so comfortable among them?

Perhaps it was our differences that made us compatible. We didn't even try to understand each another. No one in Asian neighborhoods—or in Asia itself—got mad when they couldn't "figure me out."

The more I thought about it, the more it made sense: misunderstandings were the cause of most conflicts. Why try so hard to *relate* to everyone?

Maybe it was better to maintain a sense of mystery, or a friendly indifference.

16

IN SEOUL, I was supposed to get the hometown tour from my ex-girlfriend's mom, but my attempts to figure out Korean payphones were futile—they may as well have been particle accelerators.

That was a bit of a relief, because she'd always hated me anyway. Chalk it up to cultural differences, but she was convinced that what I wrote was porn.

If only the things that people thought about us were true! Our lives would be so much more exciting than they really are. As it was, I'd been too preoccupied back then to get much writing of *any* kind done. Her daughter was the one with the real gift for using X-rated words.

The funny thing was that all the Korean films and Korea Society lectures I'd gone to hadn't given me the slightest inkling of what life was like in Seoul. The focus was always on North Korea or the DMZ. I'd seen a ton of footage of Pyongyang, rare as it is—and mostly of parades—but not a single photo of Seoul, Korea's biggest city. When it came to South Korea, I was completely clueless. I had no idea what made it tick.

The answer, seemingly, was coffee and fried

chicken. The number of places selling one or the other was staggering. The latter were open later, so that's where I ended up at four in the morning, hopelessly and painfully lost. I was earning the new faux-Native American nickname that Jeff Matika had bestowed upon me, "Sits With Book." In this case, Mike's suggestion was even more apt: "Walks Without Map."

Yes, the lively streets of Seoul that had so enamored me had disappeared along with my footprints in the snow. The dark alleys had beckoned me, then the deserted parks—followed closely by the warehouse districts and the railyards. By the time I'd decided to return to the hotel, I couldn't find any recognizable landmarks, only a seemingly infinite stretch of car dealerships with a few chicken dealerships tucked in between.

This was the end of the road for me: a snow-covered roadie on a tour of fried chicken dives, my life now just an endless succession of breasts and legs. I sat in each joint for half an hour before moving on to the next, and could detect no discernible difference—they all blurred together like one long drive. When morning finally arrived, I made one more desperate, last-ditch attempt to find the hotel, and succeeded at last. It had been right across the street the whole time.

When I awoke it was already afternoon and my head felt like someone was standing on it. The inevitable tour-induced sickness had arrived, and it was about time, since I'd done every stupid thing I could to bring it on. At this point, it wouldn't be fatal—not to my health, nor to the nerves of my traveling companions, who couldn't be expected to put up with a sneezing, wheezing roadie for more than a week. Six days were all we had left.

Food poisoning was the only ailment I'd really worried about on this trip, Jews being known more for their wry wit than their iron constitutions. Luckily, it was my sinuses that had taken the hit, not my stomach. Still, I decided to take the day off to rest up. Nestled in a warm cafe, I cracked open my latest thriller, *A Difficult Road: The Transition to Socialism in Mozambique*. By the time lobby call came, the charismatic leader had already been assassinated and a foreign-funded rebel army was moving on the nation's capital.

With my mind in a historical mood, I decided to approach one of Green Day's bodyguards when we arrived at the show. I had some burning questions—questions of a nature different than you might guess from my previous description of the bodyguards as nameless, neckless apes. The truth was not so simplistic. Goons they were, but intelligent, articulate ones, and two out of three actually had quite prominent chins. I'd been unfair, and let my imagination and assumptions carry me away. It was the same with the photographers and the crew: the temptation to paint them with a wide brush was hard to resist, but inaccurate. Their annoying qualities as people—in distinction from the work they did—were on par with mine, except in a few extreme cases.

Of the three bodyguards, Eddie, the head of security, was by far the most aloof. He came across as haughty and unapproachable, with a mile-wide chip on his shoulder. George was brusque but down-to-earth. Mehdi, much larger in size than the others, was a tender little kitten.

George was British; Mehdi, Iranian; and Eddie, Salvadorian. George was the one who may or may not have worked for contractors in Iraq; that was the question I lacked the guts to ask, because how could I even speak to him if the answer was yes? It was difficult enough to muster up the confidence to broach a subject with Eddie that was both more complicated and more sensitive: El Salvador's civil war.

I knew that nine times out of ten, touchy subjects were the ones people wanted to talk about most. That's the way it is for me, at least. Everyone is scared to bring up what I'm dying to discuss—precisely because the issues are sensitive, because they are pressing, because they weigh on my mind and heart. But my issues are primarily personal in nature, quite different from a national conflict that left nearly a hundred thousand dead.

After the war, US newspapers hardly mentioned El Salvador again. Reading them, you would think the world was just an endless succession of armed conflicts and natural disasters without cause or resolution, except for the occasional ironic ending in which the US has the last laugh. What I wanted was a follow-up: how the country had fared *after* the war, and what it was like at present.

I found Eddie in the catering room of the venue,

eating alone. When I invited myself to join him, he waved to a chair. "It's a free country," he seemed to say. But when I asked about El Salvador, he perked up noticeably, pleased to discuss something other than security.

I'd been told not to be too put off by Eddie's cold front; everyone assured me that he was friendly and talkative when given the chance. Right off the bat, I could see they were right. But I'd also been warned that most Salvadorian emigrants were extremely partisan about the war, depending on which side they had backed and the reasons for their exile in the aftermath. Eddie's smoothness and the fact that he was well educated made me suspect that he was from the well-off, politically reactionary Salvadorian elite.

My presumptions, as usual, were far off the mark. For Eddie, the war *was* a personal issue. His family and friends had fought on both sides, sometimes brother against brother. But in the years since the truce, everyone had shared the same sense of hopelessness. They were glad the war was over, but nothing had been resolved. El Salvador's problems, Eddie said, were still primarily economic, with no end in sight.

I was glad to break the ice with Eddie, to get his perspective while getting to know him a little better at the same time. It was engaging, as all interactions should be. That was refreshing, since conversation with the Green Day guys was starting to wear a little thin as the tour entered its second week. We'd exhausted our store of shared experiences, and I'd run out of prying questions to ply them with. The silences got longer as everyone receded into their shells—except for Mike, who had no shell, having left it behind in Cedar Rapids on the first tour along with his hair and sleeves.

There were aspects, even whole eras, of my life that they knew nothing about, but those subjects never came up. That's the way it is with old friends: they rarely delve into each other's lives except where their lives intersect. They talk about old times, and wrack their brains for mutual acquaintances to discuss. Otherwise, they don't ask much. That was frustrating with Green Day, but it didn't become a serious problem because facing new experiences together kept us from being hopelessly mired in the past.

The lack of loquaciousness wasn't helped by the band's sudden turn to sobriety. Since Hong Kong they'd been sipping juice instead of brew, which cut down on the heart-to-heart talks. Just like on old tours, they binged and then purged—but they had an odd reason for it now: they were performing at the Grammys in two weeks. "The cameras add fifteen pounds," Mike explained to me as he paced the catering spread, seeming stressed. "Dehydration brings out muscle tone." Already, he looked like someone had taken a vacuum cleaner to his cheeks.

Eddie had finished his dinner and left. I was in the corner of the catering area, playing the espresso machine like a pinball game, racking up the high score. Mike picked out a bottle of kombucha and an apple from among the piles of rich pastas and desserts. He was in a mood, ranting about something that had gone wrong. I nodded enthusiastically while beating a hasty retreat. Never mind quitting drinking—the man could lose fifteen pounds from worrying alone.

I wandered down the echoey corridors, flashing my pass and following the arrows to the dressing room. Inside, I found a surprisingly tender and homey scene. Jeff Matika was stretching his strings. Jason Freese was practicing tying knots while watching an instructional knot-tying video on his laptop. Tre was catnapping on the couch. "The seven o'clock slump!" he opened his eyes to announce.

Seven o'clock was the Witching Hour, the dead zone in between soundcheck and show, when everyone ambled around with nothing to do. Tonight, though, the slump felt ambient instead of anxious. Tinny music wafted from the tape deck, so faint that I was unable to confirm my fear that it was the Doors. Various crew and local event staff passed by in the hall, looking like extras in a play.

Then one by one, recognizable voices came from offstage, their bodies arriving after a lightning-to-thunder delay. The doorway framed each person as they passed, catching their image—and their essence—like a giant photobooth.

Tre sat up to watch, alert as always to any dramatic scene.

First came Bill Schneider with his briefcase.

Then Micah Chong, the bass tech, with his tool chest.

Doug the tour manager was next, with a box of Girl Scout cookies from his month-long supply. He paused for a moment (Doug only pauses, never stops) to offer each of us one. With his lanky frame and bug-eyes, he looked like a hesher speed freak, though he'd never touched drugs. He traveled with Green Day, dreaming about the day he'd get to tour instead with AC/DC.

He, too, came and went in a flash.

I sipped my espresso while munching on cookies and enjoying the preshow show. Who would be the fourth and last shot on this strip?

Just then Jason White duckwalked by, giving us a mile-wide grin.

17

DUSK IS FALLING and Korean Green Day fans stroll around in pairs or alone, catching a reflective or romantic moment before the show. It's a great place for a concert, not on the outskirts of the city, but right in the heart of Seoul, in the middle of a massive, heavily forested park. Right across from the stadium is an ancient, medieval-looking castle surrounded by a moat.

The castle grounds are unguarded and nearly empty. Against the hundred-foot walls, the strollers look picturesque and stark. The feeling is meditative and magical. It's the perfect place for a kiss.

At least one couple seems to have that in mind. First they pause to gaze over the castle's ramparts. The moat water is shimmering with the first light of the waxing moon. Then they walk slowly over the stone steps of the wide footbridge. On the other side, a band is waiting with some of the sweetest, sappiest serenades ever played. The tickets they hold are just place markers for each other's hands, and the promise of the pleasures yet to come!

So why the long faces and the nervous over-the-shoulder glances? Because everywhere they turn, some creepy roadie-looking guy is shadowing their every move. First he's skulking around the castle like Frankenstein, then he's speaking gibberish to the old man selling glowsticks outside the gig. He almost knocks them down running to cut the line at the free coffee truck, as if free coffee trucks are something unusual, not something outside *every* show, or why would anyone even go?

The night only gets worse. The first band has no shirts. Instead, they wear guitars which they hardly even play. Every song begins and ends the same: "Alright, Korea!"

When Green Day comes on, the singer repeats a word of Korean over and over, but his pronunciation leaves the would-be couple puzzled. The maddening part is that despite the singer's baby-like babble, the girl is gazing at him dreamily, as if he were food.

The guy turns away, only to spot someone in the audience having an epileptic fit. He runs over to help, and is instead pulled into a pile of people writhing on the floor. Much to his horror, he finds his limbs entangled with those of the Frankenstein guy he's been trying all night to escape.

Meanwhile, Green Day have pulled onstage an audience volunteer: who else but his date? The singer offers her an innocent peck on the cheek, but she gives him her tongue—and why not? That's what every other girl they've pulled onstage has done.

Another ruined romance, but this one wasn't my fault. At least, give me a chance to explain.

It's true about the glowstick guy. He looked tired, like he'd already worked at least one job that day. Actually, he looked like he'd woken at dawn to water the crops, then moved to the city around noon and taken a job at a factory. Now he was hawking blinking neon wands to make a little extra money to bring home to feed his family. He had a rural look, with red dirt still clinging to his shoes. That clashed with the blinking toys draped from his arms and the ones he waved halfheartedly in his hands. To suit the occasion, most of them were green.

For him, the concert was a job, just as it was for the other vendors, ticket-takers, pickpockets, and street sweepers who never got within a mile of the band. Green Day were so huge that they touched people's lives who would never even hear their songs. The funny thing was that the members of Green Day were just as far removed, although they were the main attraction of the show. Backstage and onstage they were isolated and alone. They didn't see the overflowing bike racks in front of the stadium in Seoul or feel the anticipation of the crowd queuing up to get in. I couldn't nudge them to look at the couples making eyes at each other or tease them about how the glowstick guy looked like a human Christmas tree as a result of the band name they'd hastily picked.

To be honest, it felt fucked up. While they sat backstage making millions, the glowstick guy stood in the snow, watching all the while for the cops, for an *official* vendor he was not. I wished I could give him a handful of Green Day's money so that he could get out of the cold and go home to his kids, but it had been years since I'd carried the band fund, evidently for good reason. Maybe there was something else I could get him from backstage: food, drumsticks, commemorative plaques? My offer was, predictably, lost in translation.

As for the coffee truck, it is correct to say that there was one parked outside the concert, but not that I was hysterical about it or driven to joyful tears. I calmly questioned a few people to make sure that my understanding of the situation was accurate. Free coffee and plum pastries? Yes. Fine. In an orderly fashion, I waited in line.

When "Rock 'n' Roll Radio" came over the loudspeakers, the first twenty rows were already leaping up and down like spawning salmon, but that was to be expected. All hell broke loose when Green Day came out. The audience *did* seem to be particularly wild, but to say it had anything to do with the free coffee would be jumping to conclusions. They probably just took Billie's Korean greeting to heart, and responded in kind.

Even the glowstick seller must have been pleased, for it was evident he'd sold every item in his stock. Glowsticks were among the many items prohibited inside the venue, but half of the audience must have hid them in their socks, for the entire balcony was lit up with a series of perfectly synchronized, color-coordinated waves, reminiscent of the footage I'd seen of North Korean parades. How I wished the band would say something about reunification—but that, I knew, was the kind of touchy issue they would avoid.

The dancing was loose and extremely jubilant, but to claim that anyone looked like he was having an epileptic fit is stretching the truth. And I may not be the most nimble guy in the world, especially on the dance floor, but to liken me to Frankenstein is downright cruel. Besides, when I started lurching, everyone around me followed suit.

Soon I was wrapped in the arms of a bunch of strangers, and their arms stayed around me for the rest of the night. They showed me their own moves: conga lines that swept through the crowd, and one where everyone crouched in a circle on the ground then leapt up at each other when the music reached a crest.

The band answered the crowd's enthusiasm with their own, making for the best show of the tour by far, and one of my favorites of all time. The passionate but polite jostling of the audience felt like the opening moments of a large book sale, the only thing I've found that matches the intensity of early eighties hardcore. The Seoul audience was also boisterous and loud, clapping on the off beats and singing along even with the guitar leads.

We danced together, we sang together, we drank from each other's drinks.

As for Billie kissing women onstage, for that I'll drop my defenses and speak direct: I was the one who it upset—and not just in Seoul, but at every show.

The problem wasn't the fact that he'd cultivated

an onstage persona, or accepted his role as a sex symbol. That was a natural aspect of performing, even for bands at the smallest basement shows. But part of being a sex symbol is being unattainable and out of reach—especially if you have a wife and kids.

I worried that every show ended with five thousand couples going home to five thousand fights; five thousand prickly guys too stubborn to admit that it was Billie Joe they were upset about.

Famous, charismatic, talented, sensitive, and rich—all these were almost impossibly unattainable qualities to compete with, and truly impossible once you added American and white. It was a cruel standard to be measured against, or to watch your girlfriend entranced by all night. Five thousand guys in each country we'd visited were beside themselves with worry and envy, thinking: "Is it Billie Joe she's dreaming about?"

It would be bad enough if Billie hadn't had a steady stream of women come up and grope him during the shows. Every time a girl got a kiss and a guy did a solo, it felt nauseatingly traditional.

And if it seemed gross to me, how did it feel to the other guys onstage? No one came up and kissed Mike and Tre.

Billie had always been the center of attention, but not necessarily the frontman. In the old days, everybody wrote songs, and the volume on everyone's microphones was the same. Now Billie was the star of the band.

Maybe that was inevitable, but I missed Mike's lyrics, and I thought Billie should reexamine his onstage approach. He was just being friendly, hugging everyone who came up, guys and girls alike. What could he do if they took it a step further—push them away?

Yes. Mace them, if necessary.

When in doubt, follow the Ramones.

I was at one of their concerts where a girl ran up and grabbed Joey's crotch. A bold move—but Joey's expression when he pushed her away was one of extreme discomfort, like anyone would feel after being attacked. He looked humiliated, hurt, and confused. Soon, the audience felt that way too. If she had kissed him, it might have been even worse.

Joey's untouchability didn't keep him from being a sex symbol in our eyes. It only made him seem human too.

18

ON OUR WAY into Osaka from the airport, I rode in a minivan with the Big Three. We watched as the snowcapped mountains gave way to dense forests of apartment buildings. Every balcony looked like a Manhattan Mini Storage unit, crammed to the brim with belongings. Clothes dried on coat hangers instead of clotheslines. That was my first view of Japan.

As the scenery unfolded so did our ongoing narrative, one completely unrelated to what we were seeing. The contrast was oddly soothing, syncing up unexpectedly like *Dark Side of the Moon* to *The Wizard of Oz.* It was Jason Freese, telling the unlikely but true tale of how his high school punk group became Joe Walsh's backing band.

The story went like this:

The former Eagles guitarist was fed up with the music establishment. He wanted to shake things up a bit. He needed fresh blood to breathe some new life into his songs.

Meanwhile Freese and his friends had a sideline as session musicians. Where else but LA would you find a teenage punk band like that? For Joe Walsh, they were a perfect fit: young and spunky, but also professional and competent.

Freese's career made him unique among the Big Three. He was well established as a backup musician long before he joined up with Green Day. Luckily, he didn't have the ego to match his accomplishments. Like most serious musicians, he just loved—and lived—to play. One could picture him onstage beaming just as brightly while jamming out to "Desperado" as he did to "Geek Stink Breath." His ambiguous appearance kept him from being typecast: with his felt hat and wraparound shades, Freese looked like the skinhead rude boy he was, but also disconcertingly like an old blind guy.

Jeff Matika and I were the only ones in the van who hadn't already been to Japan. Freese had toured Japan repeatedly with Joe Walsh and others. Jason White had been there so often that he spoke of Osaka as a home away from home.

That was comforting, since we had three days off in Osaka while the crew built up the stage and light shows. Unbeknownst to me, they'd been scaled back for the piddly ten thousand-seat arenas on the first leg of the tour. The shows—and special effects—would be twice as big in Japan.

My eyes grew wide as we wended our way into the city, but they dimmed as we drove back out again. The urban bustle and tall buildings receded into the distance. Soon we were on the very outskirts of town. As we pulled into the hotel, I could see open fields.

I was haunted by memories of being stuck for

days in rural Virginia before a show in DC; stranded in suburban New Jersey because there was nowhere to park the van on the Lower East Side; trapped in the Canadian interior with no coffee to be found.

Nightmares of tours past. Jason White saw them in my eyes and waved the dark clouds away. "The subway's just a few blocks from here," he reassured me. "I'll show you, just as soon as we stash our bags."

Green Day had stayed at the same hotel on their previous visits to Osaka, so Jason knew the area well. He'd probably explored it more thoroughly in recent years than he had Berkeley. On their rare breaks from touring, Jason was so glad to be home that he tended to stay in the house, with his cat by his side and the curtains drawn.

Who could blame him? After a week and a half on the road, I was beginning to burn out. For everyone else, this Asia trip was just one tiny leg of a tour that lasted on and off for two and a half *years*.

Jason led the way through backstreets and between-building shortcuts. He confidently navigated the complicated subway system and the crowded marketplaces where we emerged. He dragged me through the city like a parent carrying a kid, or a dogwalker coaxing a lazy cur. He was unusually animated, obviously excited to be on familiar yet foreign territory, and I was happy just to take it all in.

The city was buzzing with life—more so, dare I say, than even Manhattan. The people we passed were more diverse and less conservative than I'd expected from Japan. Not only were there promenading kids in ornate, overdone *Fruits*-style outfits, but also absent-minded professor types on bikes with hair sprouting out of their ears. A wide array of people made up the parade, including a fishmonger whose nasal voice made him sound exactly like Bob Dylan.

A light rain began to fall, and Jason pulled me into a dank, five-seat hole-in-the-wall to sample the local delicacy, octopus balls. Despite some misgivings—and the memory of Tre's recent meal still on my mind—I tried them, and found them delicious.

Jason had been talking up Osaka for days, and he was right: it was a riveting yet comfortable city.

Our friendship had stretched over two decades, but it had always been set in places where I had the upper hand. Even on tour with his old band, I was the one who knew my way around most of the towns. This reversal of our roles gave me the chance to see him in a new light. Sure, Jason was a copilot type, but he shined when given the opportunity to make his own program instead of just going along with the show.

As for myself, I was a little hazy from my sickness and the flight. There was something else, too, that was troubling me: the feeling that I'd been experiencing things faster than I could process them emotionally.

Living entirely in the moment had always led me to bad decisions, and later to nostalgia and regret. I'd had whole years that were so hectic I never once stopped to take stock. Nowadays I tried to step aside and get a bird's eye view of the scene, or storm, before it passed.

I could feel the tour, and my time with these old pals, quickly slipping away. I wanted to pause and think about all that had happened before it was too late. I didn't want to get back home and have to explain it to other people before I had a chance to reflect on it all myself.

Writing was my way of thinking, and for that I needed a bright and private place. Luckily, I had brought along my knapsack with my scrawled tour diary inside. It would do me good to look it over while we were still on tour, before my frame of mind changed.

So after crisscrossing the city several times with Jason, I slipped away and found a cozy little cafe. In a corner, I set up court. It was relatively quiet, open all night, and the proprietor was my favorite kind: either completely apathetic or blind. He ignored my attempts to order coffee as well as my frantic arm-waving gestures to signal for more. Instead he brought coffee to my table—and food on two occasions—according to his own schedule and his own judgment of my needs. Whatever I paid, he accepted, without giving me change.

For the whole time we were in Osaka, I sat there through most of the daylight and half of the night without evoking any comment from him, or complaint.

For the sake of our story, let's call him Dad. I did.

I'd brought along plenty of dense books on this trip, but none more difficult to get through than the one I'd written myself. My mind and mood had shifted countless times in the course of the tour, but my handwriting was consistently illegible. Even when I could make out the words, they didn't tell me anything worthwhile.

Finally I put the journal aside and sat like a hungover detective, searching my mind for clues. If I could only add up what was missing and figure out the rub, I would solve the mystery and uncover the murderer. But, of what—my youth?

Around me sat the oddest collection of cafe society. One regular customer looked like a barbarian, dressed head to toe in furs that appeared homemade. He spoke—and smoked—with a man in a three-piece suit. At another table were a group of women who looked like they'd just returned from a swank velvet-rope club. Still others came and went, types who either defied description or left no impression whatsoever, like spooks. An air of secrecy permeated the place, similar to the drug-addled and CIA-worried underworld of the Berkeley coffeehouses in which I'd come of age. Everyone spoke in discreetly low tones and avoided each other's eyes. I glanced up from time to time from my ever-growing piles of scrawled notes, only to see that no one was aware that I was there, or even alive.

I was jealous of those who could think without a pen and paper, but for me there was no other way. I played the scraps against each other like solitaire, laying them out in lines and stacking them on top of each other when they seemed to align. They read like poetry, or nursery rhymes. For instance:

Joey Ramone's butt

Al drives the diaper truck
Winnipeg skinhead
Offspring million-dollar check.

These shorthand notes were the stray hairs that stuck out awkwardly yet refused to go away. They, too, were part of the evidence in the confusing courtroom in which everyone kept trading places. That was the problem with trying to find anyone guilty or prove their innocence: every time I thought I'd gotten the story straight, something else came along that fucked up my case. It wasn't just the new experiences that had piled up, but all the ancient recollections which they brought to the surface. *That* was what I wanted to stay on top of. Otherwise they would escape, probably never to return again.

I wanted to rip up my journal and start over with just the extraneous stuff. If the exception proved the rule, then the parts of the story that didn't fit were likely to contain the real point. People were the same way; it was only after they'd told you everything about themselves that you could find out what they were actually like.

When everything fit into a neat little narrative, it stopped resembling real life. The Green Day story the mainstream press told was a perfect example: it was a nice little folktale, free of the meddlesome details that didn't contribute to the myth.

"The club that launched Green Day." What a laugh! Billie and Mike went there every week, but Gilman wouldn't even let them play. It wasn't until Al joined the band that they were allowed onstage. He had the right friends, I guess.

The underground media version of them selling out was also oversimplified. The community they were accused of betraying hadn't always treated them so well in the first place. No one, least of all Green Day themselves, mentioned that Lookout Records had ripped the band off for half a million bucks! Lookout's latter-day owners pissed away the cash—and the label's legacy—on public relations agents and full-page ads in *Spin* instead of paying the bands or sticking to their underground roots.

While Green Day's motivations and decisions were scrutinized—and rightly so—there were many other bands and businesses who were much more ambitious, and much more unsavory. Yet they were never called into question or held accountable for their actions, because they were "independent." The fact that they were failures, for the most part, no doubt helped.

Lookout cofounder David Hayes bellyached about never getting paid for the Green Day logo he'd created. Why complain? *His* rent was being paid by the unauthorized Operation Ivy bootlegs he put out. Green Day sent him a fat check anyway, and that shut him up. They may have sold out, but they'd never robbed anyone.

It was a double standard: Green Day got crucified while everyone else's sins were overlooked. They were seen as a symbol instead of a group of real people. Even decades later, that's what seemed to bother them most.

When Billie got upset by a recent book on Bay Area punk, it was because he was mentioned only in relation to his band—not as a person, or a fan.

"I *danced* at those shows!" he told me one night on tour, almost in tears. For him that was the whole point—one which no one seemed to understand. That was the kind of detail that was easily overlooked.

Yes, the crux of the story was in the fine print, not the headlines. It was in the background of the pictures and in the seemingly unimportant or unrelated anecdotes.

I didn't want to make the same mistake of rounding out the rough edges too much—neither in my mind, nor in print. For instance, my characterization of Al was only partially true. He *did* have more options than his bandmates, but he was also the one who saved up for tour by driving a diaper delivery truck—a worse job, indisputably, than Mike's gig gutting fish. Billie was the one who never seemed to have steady work.

Even the story of Billie and Joey Ramone's butt was telling. It took place at one of the first music awards shows that Green Day attended. The Academy welcomed them the same way Gilman had: by either ignoring them or treating them like little kids. But Billie was thrilled because he got a seat right behind his hero, after whom he'd named his first child.

When it came time to announce the Album of the Year, the MC paused dramatically. Billie leaned forward in his seat, and in a stage whisper, let it slip: "The Ramones!"

Joey was so disoriented that he almost stood up. The sudden rush down the aisle of Whitney Houston brought him to his senses. He turned around, but Green Day didn't even register on his radar. "Just one more voice in my head," he must have assumed.

Neither Green Day nor the Ramones were winning anything back then. They didn't stand up until the end of the show. Billie seized the opportunity to snap a picture of Joey's butt, resplendent in sagging cashmere pants. He brought it to me, knowing I would cherish it, which I did. It hung on my wall for years.

It took a long time for Green Day to become part of the rock 'n' roll pantheon. At first it was just the washed-up punks who crawled out of the woodwork to try to claim a bit of Green Day's fame. That led to some odd meetings, like one drunken night that ended with Billie gripping Wattie from the Exploited by the shaven sides of his head.

"Look into my eyes," Billie told him. "*This* is what you'll see when you die."

What he meant by that, even Billie himself wasn't quite sure—but if Wattie has a TV in his hospital room, it's as likely as not to come true. The only show Green Day hasn't been on is *Sesame Street*. When offered, they declined. "Let kids be kids," they decided.

And if guilt was being doled out—Jewish or otherwise—I had plenty of my own to contend with, and my own secrets to disclose. At one Winnipeg show, a skinhead kept coming onstage and grabbing the mic. I grabbed him and jumped into the audience—not once, but again and again, until the crowd moved away and we were hitting the concrete floor. Finally, I screamed: "Stay off the fucking stage!"

He was like, "Oh, okay."

Both our faces were streaked with blood. That's when I realized that I was getting a little macho and carried away. Being a roadie could easily turn into a power trip, getting off on pushing and bossing people around.

And though I never got paid for being Green Day's roadie, I did take money from a different successful group without doing any work to deserve it. Strange to say, but one day cleaning my room I found a million-dollar check from the Offspring. I skipped all the way to the bank.

We'd been friends, though just in passing, when they were still a small, TSOL-obsessed punk band. After their Bay Area shows, we would go bowling at an all-night place in Pinole. They must have stopped by my annual laundromat party one year, for what else would explain the birthday card I unearthed?

In 1987, the idea of punk millionaires was inconceivable, and the new century seemed impossibly far away. As a joke, they made out a check for a million dollars and wrote 2000 as the date.

Good timing—I found it in 1999.

I hoped they would take the whole thing in good humor after the initial shock. Honestly, I planned to give them back every penny if the check went through. It didn't. As a result, we can deduce that the Offspring are not millionaires. Noodles, if you're reading this, I apologize. Return to the laundromat when you get the chance.

Ah, these scraps of paper and scraps of memories. What did they add up to? What story did they tell? They were disjointed, erratic—yet they captured the essence of the changes we'd been through better than my journal of the tour.

That was the fun stuff. Other unearthed memories were disturbing, like what took place after the skinhead incident in Winnipeg. Leaving the show, a girl was raped. Before abandoning her, the perpetrator took her Green Day t-shirt.

That was something we all felt sick about. That was the dark side of your music reaching a wider audience and becoming part of people's lives.

Two people had died leaving shows by my own band, but that was different: those were accidents. Rape happens even at small shows, I know, but I took the Winnipeg incident as a warning sign that the band was getting too big, and it was all spinning out of control.

There was more, much more: scraps of paper piling up on my table as fast as I could write. Once the floodgates opened, the waters raged.

Mike shits on car

Mike cuts down trees

Windows smashed by roadies with bowling ball

Roadies kidnapped by Canadian cuties

Punks saved from angry Chicano gang by Billie

Pinhead Gunpowder

Tre instructs me on matters of hygiene.

I sat every night in the cafe wading through it all, trying to fit the pieces into the text I'd already written, the frantic record of events I'd jotted down right as they were taking place. It wasn't a matter of improving the story, because the tangents only served to slow it down and lead it off course. But it was a personal goal of mine to reconcile who and where we'd been with what we had become. For that, it was necessary to look at the fullest picture possible and tell the not always pleasant truth.

Yet I had only a few nights at that little cafe in Osaka, not years.

Someday, maybe Green Day would invite me along again and I could weave the rest into another narrative.

But who knows what else would rise to the surface by then?

19

TOURING WAS FUNNY: you reveled in all the new experiences, which came so fast that the weeks felt like months, yet the moment a semblance of regular daily life presented itself, you seized it and felt immediately soothed. Maybe that was why hooking up was such a common part of being on tour: it fulfilled the need for connection and home when you were rootless and transient yourself. It probably had as much to do with the domestic urge as it did sex. Then again, sex had a lot to do with the domestic urge, too.

But there are different kinds of homes and different kinds of settling down. It just so happened that the cafe in Osaka satisfied most of my needs. Sitting there gave me a sated, settled feeling of peace, comparable to other kinds of pleasures.

Though we were only in Osaka for half a week, we all fell into what felt like a well-worn routine. When they left to soundcheck at the stadium, I went to the cafe to write. Every night, they hung out at the same hole-in-the-wall bar. When I got off work I went to join them for a drink.

Whenever I arrived at the cafe, my table was

empty, though there was no indication it had been saved. I waited until late at night to leave, when the cafe's proprietor—and sole employee—was asleep. Around midnight, he began to doze behind the counter. His body moved forward ever so slowly, like the hands on the dusty clock, until finally his face lay flat against the cash register. The keys made small, round indentions on his cheeks.

That's when I tiptoed to the door—but he always awoke at the last minute and caught me trying to sneak out. The way he shook his head disapprovingly left no doubt he was displeased, even disgusted, but whether it was because I'd stayed too long or was leaving too soon, I was never sure. I arrived earlier each subsequent day, just in case.

Leaving the cafe, I made my way through the dark streets in a state of bliss. Footsteps on wet pavement late at night in a foreign country—the sound was like hearing angels sing. Passing thousands of strangers I'd almost certainly never see again—that, too, gave me a wistful, inexplicable sense of serenity. Neon signs shined through the rainy mist. I laughed and sang to myself as if drunk. Then I ducked into the tiny tavern that Green Day had adopted, where I usually found them in a similar state.

I could count on a chorus of greetings, a bunch of arms wrapped around me, and a few sloppy kisses on the cheek. They were Californians through and through, without that East Coast reserve that I'd become accustomed to.

After a long stretch of writing, I was even kind of easygoing myself, rather than the haunted, hunted Aaron most people knew. Working out my thoughts and emotions on the page left me relieved and made me feel complete. It provided a unity of spirit and purpose that was otherwise rare in life.

So accustomed was I to the predictable routine, it completely threw me one night when I ducked into the bar and found it empty and devoid of life. The room was silent except for the creak of the stool on which a solitary customer perched. Behind the counter, the bartender was slowly flipping through records, having a hard time deciding what to play.

"Green Day?" I asked desperately.

He shook his head. No requests?

I tried again. "No English," he said.

I immediately regretted all the mime jokes I'd once made. Trying to communicate with body language was incredibly difficult. The whole San Francisco troupe would have gotten a good laugh at my expense, watching me make an ass of myself in Osaka while attempting to play charades. I was in a panic, suddenly aware of the late hour. I didn't know how to get back to our hotel without first retracing my steps all the way back to the cafe.

The bartender waited until I'd finished, then shrugged his shoulders apologetically. Not only did he speak Japanese, he also *thought* in Japanese. Our ideas were bound to be different, as well as the gestures we would use to express them.

After I had gone through my repertoire of impressions, the woman sitting at the bar turned towards me.

"Want to use my phone?" she asked. Her English was flawless.

I thanked her profusely and called Bill Schneider. From the sound of it, he was in the middle of a riot. The crew, he said, were having a party at a different bar just a short walk away. The band had gone to join in. He gave me directions, but after hanging up, I couldn't make heads or tails of them.

"I know the place," said the woman when I handed back her phone. "If it is alright, I will join you."

Soon I was back on the streets I already felt romantic about, but now with an attractive woman by my side. Her teeth were crooked, mine were fake. It looked like a date, though I tried to ignore that feeling and push the thought from my mind. That was made difficult by the low, guttural noises she made. Like many Koreans and Japanese, she used grunting sounds as part of her speech—but in her case, they were extreme.

"Unhh!" she said, as if impaled. "Yes, I visited Guam once."

It was as if I were buried deep inside her rather than just walking by her side down the street.

"Guhh!! I have friends in San Francisco."

The intimate sounds belied the fact that, due to our cultural differences, we could barely carry a conversation. By the time we came to the second bar, we had run out of things to say.

Inside, the party was in full swing. The crew were acting uncharacteristically affectionate and sweet, having imbibed the few drinks necessary to warm them up to the level of normal human beings. Their guards were down, but the lively gleam in everyone's eyes did not come from alcohol alone. Everyone on the tour was there together, having a good time. The feeling of communion was aided by the fact that the bar was so tiny that it was impossible to avoid the dance floor. Even the shyest members of the crew were tapping their feet and rattling their limbs to the reggae coming over the sound system, slowly edging their way out of the corners they'd been hiding in.

Green Day's videographer rub-a-dubbed through the crowd. The sound guy swayed like a wounded bear. Jason Freese skanked alongside three Japanese businessmen who'd gotten caught up in the action while trying to cross the room.

Green Day's Japanese booking agents were there too. Unlike their equivalents elsewhere in Asia, the promoters from "Creative Man"—all women—were not too staid to get drunk and cut the rug. My would-be date was dancing too, as was the tailor, Kris, whose seamstress mother had trained her in the trade. The party was not entirely dudes, though alcohol did bring out the raucous, boyish aspects of the crew, as was evident by the melee that soon erupted in the men's bathroom.

It started accidentally enough. Micah Chong happens to be one of those guys who gets playfully violent when drunk. Jeff Matika is one of those innocent types who always gets hurt.

Me? I'm the kind who starts trouble, then is nowhere to be found when the shit goes down. I was the one who banged on the stall door while Micah was doing his business, but by the time he finished I was clear across the bar enjoying a cold beer.

Jeff Matika limped out first with bruised ribs and a nearly fractured wrist. Kenny the drum tech emerged next, demonstrating the definition of "nebbish" (the schlemiel trips over the schlemazel and lands on the nebbish). He staggered onto the dance floor with a gash over his left eye.

It was when Mike took over in the DJ booth that the whole place really went apeshit. From Mike I expected Otis Redding or the Who, but the records he chose were all scathing, straightforward punk. I had no idea he actually listened to that kind of stuff. It made me reconsider something that had been on my mind ever since the show in Seoul, when a magazine devoted to Green Day made the rounds backstage.

"THREE PUNKS WHO CHANGED THE WORLD" read the headline. Something about it rubbed me wrong. Were Green Day punks? That's what I couldn't figure out.

Billie was; he'd recorded and released records by other bands, thus completing the cycle of support. With Tre and Mike, it was harder to say. They'd gone to punk shows and played in punk bands, but so did a lot of people, without ever really committing themselves or getting involved. Perhaps Tre and Mike had never really felt included, or never wanted to be, preferring to remain outsiders even in a scene of people who didn't fit in.

Yet of the three Green Day members, the one who'd written the most enduring punk anthem was actually Tre: "Outside," by the Lookouts, his first band. It was about distancing yourself from the crowd.

"Never mind those bastards on the sidewalk
I don't mind them shouting things at me
Never mind the way they talk, I don't care
Let them talk about me..."

Too bad Tre had cast himself as the band clown in Green Day. He still had plenty of anger and alienation left in him, and humor wasn't the best way to express it. Unlike Mike, Tre wasn't actually a particularly funny guy. They both seemed trapped in the images they'd created, Tre as a joker and Mike as serious and tough. Tre's songs in Green Day were all tongue-in-cheek, and all of Mike's humor came out offstage.

That was a shame, but beside the point, which was: were Green Day punks?

In an active sense they weren't, but in a private sense they were, inasmuch as punk had affected their lives deeply enough to remain an integral part. I remembered how pleased Tre was when he found a Gilman Street in Hong Kong and took a photo underneath the sign, though it had been ages since he'd gone to Berkeley's Gilman Street for a gig.

But what surprised me more was how obviously,

genuinely moved by the music they still seemed. Mike acted as if the records he played were a natural extension of his own deepest feelings and moods. Tre too; he was so excited that he picked me up from where I stood and lovingly lobbed me halfway across the room. All those years of pounding the drums had made him deceptively, almost frighteningly strong.

As if to answer my burning question, everyone in the place started to thrash.

The table I landed on flipped over. The bar's staff, made up of Japanese versions of Johnny Thunders and Joan Jett, were nonplussed. Perhaps the heroin here was of a finer grade? Soon every table was flipped over and pushed out of the way.

Punks or not, we were all together in the pit, including Mike, who would miraculously emerge from the whirlwind to put on another angry anthem just as the last one came to an end. I'd been dancing every night of the tour, but not like this. It brought me back to my preteen days—not at gigs, where I was too shy to enter the fray, but in basements where we killed the lights and put on *This Is Boston, Not L.A.*

It was pure bliss, without irony or embarrassment. Being in motion with your friends, crashing and being crushed against them, was one of the purest feelings in the world. It was also one of the hardest to come by as everyone got older, grumpier, and less active. I certainly hadn't expected to find it in Japan with Green Day.

Yet it felt as natural as could be. Eighties punk

was our native soil, our mother's milk, regardless of the different ways we related to it and the different directions our lives had taken in the decades since. What we still had in common was greater than our differences, or so it seemed in Osaka as we flew through the air or found ourselves flat on our faces on the floor. We were like landsmen from a country that no longer existed, performing the old rituals and finding that they still made sense and still spoke meaningfully to our needs.

This was the Green Day I loved: tangled up in a pile on the floor, with me underneath. What other old friends of mine still danced in public, and were still unafraid to embarrass themselves? Only Eggplant came to mind. He would have enjoyed this.

Mike extricated himself from the pileup but let the needle spin in the grooves at the end of the disc. There was a momentary lull while everyone dusted themselves off and attended to their injuries. Billie motioned to me to join him on the dance floor. Over the speakers came the notes that never fail to give me goosebumps: the opening chords of the greatest song of all time, "Kiss Me Deadly" by Generation X.

Dancing in the middle of a maelstrom was different than with just one person in the center of the room. I deferred, but Billie knew me better than that. "*Please* drag me out onto the dance floor" is what I really meant.

He did, and everyone else gave us space.

I'd needed to shake off the self-consciousness and lethargy that had come to me with age. Touring with

Green Day had been great for that, because I got to dance—but only to the band, not *with* them. Once upon a time, Billie and I had danced together at every show. Until now, I didn't realize how much I had missed that.

Dancing together was sexy, it was sweet. It was everything that friendship—and being on tour—should be. It was the prom night I'd never had, done right.

It was like a dream. As the song concluded, he wrapped me in his arms, leaned me over, and gave me a long and tender kiss.

I went to sleep grinning, and woke up the same way, thinking: "Goddamn if that wasn't one of the funnest fucking nights of my life!"

20

THE MORNING SUN did not catch everyone looking so pleased. Bill Schneider woke up and went out, but felt sick and went right back to the hotel to sleep. Billie didn't even get out of bed until 8:00 PM. Jeff Matika iced his swollen, nearly broken wrist. Everyone else iced their aching heads.

Tre was, as always, the exception. He was up bright and early for a date with the owner of the bar we'd just trashed. Together they caught a train to the rural area an hour outside of Osaka, where they took a long and leisurely stroll in the woods.

He'd pulled me aside in the middle of the mayhem the night before to confide his excitement about the plan, which had as much to do with nature as the fact that the bar's owner was a total fox. "I miss the country," he told me. Getting off the grid always gave him a peaceful, grounded feeling, reminding him of the hills above Willits where his parents live.

Tre was smart to escape when he did. As fantastic as the evening had been, the aftermath left us all out of sorts. It was as if the climax of the tour had already been reached and all that was left was the morning after, when you feel awkward and wish you were home in your own bed. Happy as I was when I awoke, I was already thinking of the tour in past tense.

I went to the cafe, but only because I didn't know what else to do with myself. My quest for some deeper truth had passed, as had my desire to write. I sat there feeling lost and like I'd missed my flight, which in a perfect world would have departed from a makeshift runway right behind the bar moments after Billie's kiss.

I wanted my time with Green Day to conclude on a good note, and the last notes of "Kiss Me Deadly" were as good as they got. It was a fairy tale ending, rather than the kind of last-minute blowup that could turn the whole thing into a cautionary tale instead: why you should never travel with old friends. Even if my fears of an eleventh-hour disaster were unfounded, how could things get anything but worse after a high point like that?

I was besieged by the same worries I get at the tail end of every trip, whether overseas or just to visit the in-laws. The final days always seemed to invite catastrophe. I'd been careful to avoid conflict on this tour, but I could sense that my time was up and my luck was running out. The burst of excitement at the bar, as beautiful as it was, could just as easily have been a different kind of explosion. I felt as if some terrible accident had been narrowly averted.

Suddenly I longed to be back home. The sights and sounds of tour were wasted on me. I stopped taking it all in, and began to count the days instead. The truth is, I missed my girlfriend.

Afraid of being late for lobby call, I rushed back across town, but ended up idling at the hotel with hours left to kill. Following Tre's cue, I decided to take a nature walk. Unlike the Green Day guys, I *actually* walked alone—and if anyone were around I would have said that aloud, which was a sign that I was getting edgy and had to watch my mouth.

Nearby were marshlands I'd spied from my window but had yet to explore. Upon closer inspection they turned out to be more like a toilet than a state park: a junk-strewn wasteland along a body of water fed by concrete tubes spewing out the city's puke and shit. For my mood, it was a perfect fit.

Out of habit, I sniffed around for a place to sleep. If I ever returned to Osaka I'd have to find my own accommodations, and these weren't half bad. I came across several homeless encampments whose residents didn't seem menacing, plus half a dozen uninhabited spots that were, relatively speaking, prime real estate.

It felt like at the end of a relationship, when you've already said goodbye in your mind and have started to plan the next stage of your life. The thought of returning to Osaka under different circumstances and waking up on the waterfront was comforting. I started looking forward to it.

If the "morning after" was the beginning of the end, the show later that night was the breakup sex. Instead of getting caught up in the spirit of things, I looked on with a sense of detachment and a morbid attention to detail. I busily committed it to memory, as if it were my last chance. The rigging next to the stage provided the best view, where I could watch from close up without being observed myself.

Now I was done overlooking the things that bothered me about the band. I wanted to run onstage and strangle Billie every time he yelled "Get those hands up in the air!" Did he not realize that most people's reaction was to run when they heard those words?

Yet my detachment made me more objective too, able to really appreciate the sterling qualities of what I'd had, now that I was about to throw it in the trash.

Some aspects of Green Day that had previously annoyed me, I now saw through different eyes. Their song "Minority" was a case in point. Witnessing twenty thousand Japanese sing "I want to be the minority" was as invigorating as it was surreal; quite different from when I first heard the song, sung by a bunch of redneck roofers working in a mostly black neighborhood.

Context changed everything. An audience of Asians yelling "I don't want to be an American idiot" was not the same as an audience from Long Island singing along. American was something that these folks would never be, though American values were constantly shoved down their throats and American troops still occupied their country. As a result, the song came across as more powerful in Japan, and somehow more personal as well. Another big difference here was that you could see the eyes of the audience move, but not their mouths, for at least half the crowd was wearing surgical masks. So prevalent were those mouth coverings among Japanese Buddhists that Mike had the bright idea of making some with band logos printed on them.

Turned out it had already been done.

Seeing everything like a spy was voyeuristic but cool. There were very few of my friends I'd gotten to watch from a distance or stare at without having to turn away.

Part of distancing myself was emotionally preparing for the split. I knew that even if we left off on good terms, we would probably never be like this again. We would go our separate ways and before another chance like this came along, we'd be dead.

I'd traveled with them first as a young man and now again as I approached middle age. Twice in a lifetime was lucky, thrice was extremely unlikely, considering the forces that led everyone along different paths and scattered them to the far corners of the earth. Besides, would Green Day still be a band in another twenty years, for me to travel with? That was a sobering thought.

At any rate, just because I considered them family didn't mean I'd get invited to the reunions. They were a very insular group. They hung out together even at home. I either saw them all, or none at all—and if I had a falling out with one, the rest didn't tend to return my calls.

That was the bad side of them being family-like: even if you didn't get disowned, it was easy not to be included. Often the cold shoulder treatment wasn't even intentional, but merely due to the nature of their work. They were in permanent tour mode even during the rare times they weren't on the road; that meant living in the present and dealing with only the most pressing matters at hand. Everything else—and everyone else—got shelved. People outside the pack they traveled with were "civilians," and civilians were notoriously hard to relate to.

In a few days, I would be one of those civilians again.

Soon I would be seeing Green Day on magazine covers instead of in the flesh. My perspective on them would change. In all likelihood, they would appear much worse from the outside than they did from within.

On tour, Green Day were guys I ate breakfast with every morning. In New York, they were a terrifying monster that stalked me in all-night donut shops, in supermarket checkout lines, and even on the subway. Their hype was impossible to escape. Seeing them up close made me forget the cultural behemoth they had become. Seeing them from afar made it easy to forget that they were human.

Part of me was anxious to return to daily life, where everything was not so grandiose and staged. The other part held tight to my pass, sad to lose access to my old friends.

In Osaka, the band pulled some unexpected songs out of the bag, overlooked gems from the lesser-known albums I love best. That was enough to lure me into the crowd—and not a moment too soon, for my hiding spot near the stage turned out to be where the show-ending pyrotechnics were set to go off. I would have been burnt to a crisp had I stayed there for another few minutes, or so claimed Bill Schneider, who should always be taken with a grain of salt.

Backstage, the blowout or breakup I'd spent all day bracing myself for was nowhere in sight. Everyone was in a considerate and loving mood, doting on each other the way old couples do. Everyone was gentle and humble—and back on the wagon, which no doubt helped.

The weather front had passed, or perhaps I had been seeding the clouds myself. Yet my nearly averted accident avoiding fireworks was not the only one of the day. When I asked Tre how his hot date went, he waved away my wink and nod. The response was typically Tre, but even more disturbing than I'd come to expect.

"She was too cool to do that to," he said. "You don't shit where you sleep."

Did Tre hate women, or himself—or "neither and both"? That was a phrase Milosevic, the former Serbian leader, had used to evade a particularly incriminating question during his trial at the Hague.

I decided to let someone else puzzle that one out; I was a former roadie, not a shrink.

One last thing to say about the night: it was a benefit. Green Day donated their proceeds from the show to earthquake relief in Haiti.

$100,000—that was no small take.

21

MY MOM HAD AN old friend named Bob, who I still run into from time to time in the Bay Area. Sprightly and with a gleam in his eye at age eighty-seven, Bob makes the rounds to all the cultural events and art shows. In fact, he gets around more than I do. On the bullet train to Tokyo, I thought of a story he told me years ago.

It was 1941 and Bob was a student at UC Berkeley. Every day the newspaper headlines grew more ominous. Japanese Americans saw the writing on the wall: they were unwanted, and would either be kicked out or locked up at the first excuse. The US government had chartered a steamship and was offering free passage "back to the motherland," where most of them had never even been. Bob and his parents argued about what to do: flee, or face the inevitable repression. Bob's best friend took the boat. Shortly after their tearful farewell, Pearl Harbor was bombed.

Bob and his parents were among the one hundred and twenty thousand Japanese Americans rounded up on the West Coast and put into camps. They were sent to Topaz, in the desert a hundred miles south of Salt

Lake City. Internees were allowed, even encouraged, to apply to colleges east of the Mississippi, so after a year and a half, Bob was able to leave Topaz to attend Wayne State University in Detroit. Unfortunately, he sent the camp a change of address card, which they forwarded directly to the draft board. Bob was pulled out of college yet again, this time to serve in the military.

Bob was stationed in Tokyo. He arrived in a city in total ruins, shortly after Japan's defeat, as a member of the conquering army. On a street corner, he saw a beggar dressed in rags. Their eyes met. It was his old friend.

At this point in the story, Bob paused. I waited for the punch line, but for him it had already come. "So," he went on, "did you see the exhibit of Spanish Civil War posters at the Live Oak Arts Center? And what's happening down at that Gilman Street club you were involved with?"

"What about your friend?" I pressed. "Was it awkward? Did you keep walking? Was he angry with you?"

"No, no," said Bob. "Not at all. We hugged and laughed about the way things had turned out. What can you do? We were just glad to see each other again."

Bob didn't return to Japan until 1994, to do research for an art exhibit he was setting up to commemorate the fiftieth anniversary of the dropping of the atomic bomb. He visited Hiroshima and Nagasaki. A long-delayed reparation check helped him afford the trip, for Bob had always been a man of small means. It was probably the first vacation he'd ever taken, and I remember how excited he was. As for Bob's old friend in Tokyo, he was nowhere to be found.

I knew that when our paths crossed next, Bob would question me about my own impressions of Japan. Thinking about my response, I felt ashamed. I'd been given a once-in-a-lifetime opportunity and had mostly squandered it. What could I tell Bob? That Japan was just the background for my trip, almost totally eclipsed by the ridiculous situations and overblown personalities of the band I was traveling with? That we'd stayed in the finest hotels, yet all the while I ached to be back home in my filthy bed? That I'd spent most of my time in Japan with Americans, either in bars or in total isolation backstage?

And in four days, not a single museum.

All of that was embarrassing to me, but to Bob it would probably be fascinating. He had a curious mind—and maybe a few Green Day records too, for all I knew. He'd surprised me before, not only by his ability to laugh at hardships, but by the breadth of his interests. In turn, I'd surprised him every time I recognized his voice on the phone. "Mom, call from Bob!" I'd yell. He whispered over the line: "How could you tell?"

That was easy. The most interesting people always seemed to be the most soft-spoken and least self-absorbed.

I missed having to perk up my ears to hear, or

strain my eyes to see, the way I did when walking in the forest at night or looking at an interesting piece of art in a gallery. Traveling like this, there were no subtleties. Instead of picking up impressions, all my senses were assaulted. Scenery was something I passed while I was getting chased. And people—people were something to dodge as if in an obstacle course.

Even the gestures my friends made were theatrical and exaggerated; they were accustomed to being onstage, communicating with people from thousands of feet away.

I leaned back in my seat, kneading my shoulders with my hands. My nerves were still in a knot from the near-riot at the train station, for which I'd been completely unprepared. Mehdi the bodyguard had even commented on the unusual state of affairs on our way there: "It's like an alternate universe—everyone has coffee except for Aaron."

My mistake had been thinking I could just grab a quick cup while we waited for the train. Instead, it was a mob scene from the moment we set foot in the door. Crazed Green Day fans had staked out the station, and they waited in ambush at every turn. They ran the wrong way down escalators, blocking our path. They dive-bombed from behind pillars and magazine kiosks. They reached out like zombies, trying to tear off hunks of our flesh.

One woman was crying as she chased us carrying a *newborn baby* in her arms.

It was insane, nothing like the usual airport drill—and I was still half-asleep, helpless without caffeine.

Even when we were safely aboard the train, the fans pressed so forcefully against the windows that the glass threatened to break. The ticket-taker did a quick sweep, ejecting a few stray groupies who were hiding underneath the seats.

It was enough to make you paranoid. Was the ticket-taker for real, or merely a Green Day groupie using an elaborate ruse, having murdered the *real* ticket-taker and stolen his suit? And what of the snack cart guy wheeling his cart down the aisle—could it be a Trojan horse filled with Green Day maniacs, waiting for their chance to strike?

Just as we wiped the sweat off our brows and began to relax, the train unexpectedly stopped in the suburbs of Osaka and another small army set to banging on the windows of our car. Our view was completely obscured by signs reading "Tre Cool #1" and "I love Billie Joe."

As excitable as the Japanese fans were, they were still preferable to the comparatively sedate Green Day stalkers back in the States. Those were an eerie bunch, mostly lost-looking middle-aged women and glassy-eyed teens, plus the occasional Green Day groupie family that contained both. Where the dads were, I don't know—though that may have been the point.

Armed with seemingly inexhaustible expense accounts and trust funds, they crisscrossed the country attending every single Green Day-related event. That kind of frivolousness I could understand in a once-in-a-lifetime or one-last-wish scenario, but not every single week! The decadence of it made me sick. I was grateful, and a bit shocked, that none of them had followed us halfway around the world. The Japanese fans were starstruck, but not crazy enough—or rich enough—to devote their whole lives to the band.

I felt sorry for Billie, Mike, and Tre. Being on the receiving end of all that attention had to be rough. Not only was Green Day loved by strangers, they were hated by people they'd never met. That was a lot to have to deal with.

At 180 miles an hour, the journey went fast. As we pulled in to Tokyo, I realized that my idea of the city was an odd composite of Bob's wartime story, Billie's reports of coffee vending machines on every corner, and my own reading about terrorist attacks. I could ride the train between the different extremes, dodging doomsday cults armed with deadly sarin gas.

My enthusiasm dampened somewhat when I took a peek at the subway map. It was impossibly intricate, with what seemed like thousands of different lines. Instead of a transit system, it looked like a family tree.

Though our reception was thankfully uneventful, Tokyo itself—the real Tokyo—was intimidating. Unlike Osaka, it seemed to lack the small-town charm that some metropolises retain. The feeling in the air was electrifying but not exactly inviting.

First impressions can be deceiving, especially through the window of a van. Unfortunately, there wasn't going to be time for anything but a surface impression on this trip. I decided to stick with the band for once.

Our first stop was the ominously named American Village, a neighborhood filled with small hip-hop-themed boutiques. According to Billie, the bulk of the businesses had been huge thrift stores just a few years earlier. He lamented the change.

We split up into little groups, and when we returned to the rendezvous point, Mehdi was proudly showing off his new tattoo. For a first-ever tattoo, the piece was huge, but on Mehdi's mammoth body it looked like just a little smudge.

I'd also been with the band when Mike got his first ink, if memory serves me right. He and Billie decided to make the most of a night off in Memphis by getting something they would never forget. I was at the river at the time with other pressing matters, but where Al was, I haven't a clue. It was just like us to be absent at the commitment ceremony, Al purposely distancing himself, and me with an excuse.

Now the years had passed; Mike had nearly full sleeves, and the girl I'd kissed was sending her kid off to college just as soon as the financial aid check arrived.

We went record shopping next, an unusual treat in Japan because of the national mania for obsessive collecting. Each store was like a carefully curated museum filled with the works of the great masters. Instead of cheap reproductions—shoddy reissues and bootlegs—it was breathtaking to see the originals, to look at the grooves and drool over the picture sleeves. The reggae stores had every dusty single ever recorded at Studio One. The punk stores had the complete output of even the most obscure '77 bands.

The prices were prohibitive, but that allowed me to browse without worrying over what to buy, like on a visit to a library or historical archive. I was free to pontificate instead, and step into the role I'd been training for my whole life: professor of punk. Jason White knew sixties rocksteady; Scott Pelkey, Green Day's wardrobe guy, knew Japanese hardcore. I was the authority on what came in between.

I lectured on the Outlets. I held forth about the Mice. I cautioned against the Rich Kids, who had many albums but only one good song. On that point, I was proven right, but on others Billie was wise to ignore my advice. He ended up schooling me on a few bands I'd unfairly dismissed or ignored. We all have our blind spots, and mine was the Boys. I've been listening to them every night since, trying to make up for lost time.

I excused myself when our shopping spree was finished. Because the subway intimidated me I wanted to take it, for I hate being afraid of the unknown.

I rode for a while and got off at a random stop where the neighborhood looked like a Japanese St. Marks Place. It was too crowded and touristy for my tastes, but I got a kick out of seeing some familiar artwork among the displays of bootleg shirts. One image had been lifted from an old Berkeley punk flier with a Japanese theme. Now it had been reclaimed.

Back at the hotel, a new tradition began. Gone were the days of drinking in the lobby. Let other bands live the rock 'n' roll lifestyle with groupies and bars; Green Day could now be found bent over a Scrabble board instead.

I trounced them twice before realizing that humiliating my benefactors was bad form, especially when they'd been paying for my travel expenses and hotel rooms.

Mike and Tre were competitive guys. Why not just let them win?

As it turned out, a move by Tre made any chivalry on my part unnecessary.

"Qat" on a triple word score—what more needs to be said?

22

TOKYO WAS SO IMMENSE that its suburbs stretched outward for seventy miles. At the very end of the sprawl stood what looked like a spaceship, an impossibly ugly building jutting out from amidst the otherwise low-lying terrain. Its blinking lights flashed on and off, spelling out a message: "Green Day."

In a minivan, and at that unfriendly hour of the morning, the distance seemed even longer than the trip from Osaka. I pitied all the showgoers who had to take the subway. The lengthy commute was the reason the show was a matinee: after the encore, everyone would have to run to catch the last train.

For us, a matinee meant an inhumanely early lobby call, since both bands needed to soundcheck and get settled in long before the gig began. Instead of exploring Tokyo, we would be stuck in the sticks the whole day. At least the club was such an eyesore that I couldn't lose sight of it, no matter how far I walked—or so I thought.

As the bands tuned up, I stuffed my pockets with food. A pedestrian bridge led from the parking lot into a residential area like those adjacent to most arenas and airports: lower class and a little weather-beaten. Before the war it had probably been farmland. Now it was a suburb in the 1950s style: quaint and cookie-cutterish, yet not upscale.

The further I walked, the nicer the houses got. There were creeks and fields for the kids to play in, fruit trees, softball games in the park—that kind of crap. It was the type of town I was glad not to have grown up in, but which I liked to visit as an adult when I was troubled and needed to ease my mind. A good place for a long bike ride.

It reminded me of a low-rent version of Bay Farm, the pseudo-island next to Oakland, where most of the residents are also Japanese. I'd lived there once for a couple of months. Every night I had to cross two bridges and three cities to get home. The walk was excruciatingly long, but I remember it fondly. It gave me time to think, time I sorely needed but wouldn't have otherwise set aside.

Now I was homeward bound again. After the longest two weeks in history, this was my last day. Walking along, I thought of all the things I would do and all the people I would see when I arrived back in New York. My thoughts were interrupted by passersby speaking Japanese, reminding me that I still had a long way to go.

This was my last day of the tour, but I still had seventeen hours in airports and on planes before I got home.

That was more time than I needed to think. That was a really long walk, and another one I would have to do alone. Green Day and their crew were leaving on a different flight headed south—first to one final show in Japan, then to LA to practice for the Grammys. It was going to be sad retracing my steps without them by my side.

I'd gotten used to being part of a gang. Without the excitement and the camaraderie of traveling with them, my seventeen hours would be just a long and wearisome wait.

There was something else, humiliating to admit: it would be weird to arrive at the airport and have no one chase me or ask for my autograph. Traveling with a famous band had given me an inflated sense of my own importance. I'd been the flea whispering in the elephant's ear: "Feel the bridge shake with our mightiness."

But the cheering crowds and rockstar treatment wasn't what I was saddest to leave behind—not even the swimming pools or the lavish feasts. I'd laughed louder and longer on this tour than I had in years. *That* was what I would really miss.

I found an enormous community garden on the outskirts of town and sat there watching the sun go down. Little clapboard sheds dotted the rolling hills, and I could make out silhouettes of old folks resting on the landings after a day spent working their plots. Suburbs where I came from didn't look like this.

This was the other side of touring which I was reluctant to part with: being in places that were entirely new, and surrounded by people who were completely unknown. Away from home, my senses were more highly attuned. It wasn't only strangers' conversations that didn't interrupt my thoughts, but also the writing on the billboards and signs that I passed.

There were, however, some benefits to speaking the same language as everyone around you. Try describing an arena, a rock band, and throngs of screaming fans using only your hands. Foolishly, I hadn't thought of getting the *name* of the stadium before turning my back on it.

I approached an old couple for help. Soon a whole curious crowd had gathered, gardeners in big hats still holding their tools in their hands. They stood there in the dusk, trying to make sense of my wild gesticulations. I may as well have been describing Godzilla, judging from the looks they gave.

Finally one old woman asked, "Train?"

Remembering the subway platform outside the stadium, I eagerly nodded my head. She turned me around and, to the amusement of everyone present, gave me a little nudge.

Soon the elevated subway tracks appeared in the sky. I followed them to the end of the line. There, the line for the concert began. Each new train that arrived was depositing a fresh load of Green Day fans.

When I got closer, I saw another queue snaking into the distance: the line for merch, a thousand people long!

Inside, the coat check counter was as busy as a ticket window at the racetrack. A team of workers carefully bagged up backpacks and jackets, affixing them with plastic, numbered tags. The whole thing was a phenomenally large operation, beyond the scale of anything I had witnessed besides a few huge antiwar demonstrations and Pride parades. The sheer mass of humanity was awe-inspiring; it was more of a beehive than Penn Station.

There was a rush even in the off-limits corridors deep in the bowels of the stadium; it was Green Day and their bodyguards leaving the dressing rooms to take the stage. Damn matinee shows—I hadn't realized it had already gotten that late.

I ducked into an empty room while they passed, not wanting to be seen going the other way.

While the opening chords of "21st Century Breakdown" thundered dully in the distance, I sat in the band's still-warm chairs, eating strawberries from bowls in their backstage spread. Though they were playing directly above, I found myself suddenly unable or unwilling to move. It was nice to sit for a moment in the residue of their energy—to warm myself as I would by the embers of an abandoned campfire on the beach.

I knew the drill well enough by now that I could picture the scene without watching it in person. I could visualize the audience, too. From a distance the crowd was as loud as the band, something I hadn't realized when I was in the midst of it.

Reluctantly, I got up from my seat, but only to step into the next room where Tre's warm-up drums were set up. It felt good to bang away and work up a sweat—to play music for a change instead of watching others do it. While a cast of thousands stood on deck, I imagined I was down in the hold stoking the ship.

A stowaway, crawling out of his hiding place to nibble on the crumbs of leftover food—that was more like it. A former roadie turned rodent.

Soon the shore would be in sight.

I walked down the hall, peeking into each room. Touring seemed to be a world in itself, with whole countries I'd barely seen in the course of two weeks. Dancing to the band every night, I hadn't considered that something else might be happening at the same time down below. Much to my surprise, the various offices were a flurry of activity despite the fact the band was onstage. Apparently this was when Green Day's paper-pushers really got down to business—or took their lunch breaks and goofed off, knowing their bosses weren't around to watch.

Now the "help" had the run of the house. The managers and accountants, the booking agents and personal assistants were all running or lounging around. What intrigues and romances went on down here, I wondered. By focusing on the band and the crowd, I'd missed a key part of the picture. After all, Green Day's stagehands and bodyguards were only half of the crew.

Billie's old guitar tech had made the same mistake. He'd done a whole series of fanzines about being on tour, without ever once straying from the side of the stage. Fascinating reading it was, for it unintentionally told much more about the roadie's perspective than that of the fans or the band.

But even the band's standpoint was hopelessly skewed. A bird's-eye view of the audience was deceptive; it tended to make everything appear more hectic—or more violent—than it really was. "The crowd was really going wild tonight," Mike told me after one show; I didn't have the heart to tell him it hadn't felt that way from where I stood.

Everyone had their own perspective, and each thought theirs was the clearest one. Everyone had their own methods of escape, too—their own ways of eking out a little personal space and creating their own comfort zone.

You could live backstage, like the mice-like members of the crew, without ever going upstairs to see the band. You could live onstage and never venture into the crowd. You could live on the phone like Freese and Matika, always calling your family, or in a fantasy like Doug, waiting to be rescued by AC/DC.

Or you could live in a book, like me, with your mind somewhere else half of the time.

These days I was more of a tourist than a tour guy, anyway. The touring world was an exciting place to visit, but not somewhere I wanted to live, as Green Day did.

I tried the weights in the weight room. I was thinking about an article I'd read about a jazz producer down on his luck who answered an ad in the paper and ended up as tour manager for Kiss. Every night he put the band onstage, then raced across town in a taxi to some tiny, smoky dive to hear the music he really loved. Just as the clock struck midnight, he was back to greet the sweaty ogres backstage with a rousing, "Great set!"

I'd do the same thing tonight with Green Day—but literature and history was my jazz. Who was I kidding with the gym act? I gave up on the weights and went back to my book. This was my last chance to catch up on the dusty tomes that wouldn't seem so thrilling once I arrived back home.

The roar made it oddly easy to concentrate on my reading; it was a blanket of noise that I tucked myself underneath. For once, my book—a military history of WWII—synced up perfectly with my surroundings: Tokyo, massive rallies, bunkers, hiding Jews. The Japanese army had just crossed Malaya on bikes in order to catch the British by surprise and capture Singapore. They were brutal but tactically brilliant, something the history books will never say about the United States.

It was good to be reminded that the US wasn't the only empire that had occupied every country we'd visited on this tour. Japan had been humbled in the aftermath of the war. So had Germany. They both had to find their place in the world instead of trying to control and conquer it.

Someday we would, too.

In the meantime we kept supporting our troops—unconditionally—just like Germany and Japan had.

That was an idea we needed to get past.

23

IT WASN'T ONLY the band that looked like they'd just had sex at the end of the show, but the audience too. Everyone spilled out the doors with beaming faces and ruddy cheeks. Their voices were hoarse from singing. They smelled of sweat, and more than a few had tears of joy in their eyes.

Hadn't anyone told these folks that a big, corporate concert was an alienating experience? That being *involved* in the event and not just a passive consumer was much more fulfilling?

Apparently not—and I didn't speak Japanese.

The uplifted, unified spirit of the crowd was exhilarating, but it wasn't as if I was seeing it here for the first time. Green Day had always made people happy, even at the tiny shows they used to play in Eggplant's backyard. That was what made them so special in the first place. That was why they stuck out and got noticed—and why they eventually had to leave.

Ironically, Green Day was an example of what DIY shows needed most: bands with plenty of character and catchy, memorable songs. Too bad those groups were the ones who inevitably got big, if they managed to stay together—which, of course, they rarely did.

Even if the spirit was the same as at Green Day's old Bay Area gigs, packing in the population of a medium-sized city certainly added to the thrill, especially when they all came running out of the same doors at the end of the night. Soon a river of people had formed flowing from the stadium to the subway—people as far as the eye could see.

Along the route, men wearing signboards held out handbills for Green Day drink specials and Green Day karaoke at local bars. Hawkers at makeshift stands sold bootleg Green Day goods, mostly keychains and coffee mugs with nonsensical slogans emblazoned on them. Billie got a kick out of that stuff, and kept his own collection of the weirdest items, culled from the random sampling he sent someone out to buy every week.

None of it, however, was as silly as the Green Day socks we used to make ourselves. Sometimes we had nothing but socks to sell on tour, and that lack of merchandise had resulted in at least one happy accident. In Vancouver, I growled at an eager fan, "We don't have any fucking shirts. Learn to silkscreen and make your own!"

And so she did, out of spite. Five years later she was running a successful screenprinting business and fronting her own band. I met her, for what I thought was the first time, when they came to the Bay Area on tour. It was only much later that she told me the story of how I'd been a total jerk, and how she'd taken my challenge at its word.

Yes, the hard work you do to make the world a better place mostly comes to naught, but the accidental stuff sometimes pays off.

I wondered, would the guys selling bootleg Green Day mugs tell anxious customers the same thing? There was an undeniable excitement that came from the massiveness of an arena show, but there were also airtight arguments for doing it yourself.

Inside, the stadium was empty now except for a few stragglers. I watched a kimono-clad old woman help her grandchildren into oversized Green Day outfits before they headed out into the cold. Would their culture disappear with globalization and the passing of generations? Probably it would be elastic and absorb outside influences, as it had so many times before.

A team of workers busily dismantled the barricades. Another crew armed with leaf blowers rustled the mountains of confetti that had been sprayed into the audience at the climax of the show. Colorful and fluttering through the air half an hour earlier, it was now a dirty, trampled mess on the floor.

This was my last goodbye. I watched the dream world I'd been living in get packed up and thrown in the trash. Like Cinderella's carriage, the whole facade would soon vanish into thin air.

"There you are!" cried Mike as I entered the dressing room. "We thought you had decided to stay in Japan. Which isn't a bad idea, if I do say so myself—but you promised a rematch first."

And so came to a close another chapter of our lives. On the ride back to the hotel, Billie sat next to me, checking in, as he always did these days: "You doing alright? Did you have a good time?"

My airport-bound bus left at the crack of dawn. Billie, Mike, Tre, and Jason White shared the last few hours of the tour with me huddled around a Scrabble board. It was a postshow glow of our own as we tapped our toes to the Exploding Hearts album on the stereo and drew tiles from the bag.

I'd volunteered the use of my hotel room, but that was unanimously vetoed as soon as we stepped inside. The socks I'd washed in the sink and left to dry on the electrically warmed toilet seat were part of the reason for the stench—but only part.

"The new Aaron," indeed! Eat your words, Tre.

We relocated to Mike's swank and less stinky suite, and were up all night playing.

ABOUT PM PRESS

PM Press is an independent, radical publisher of critically necessary books for our tumultuous times. Our aim is to deliver bold political ideas and vital stories to all walks of life and arm the dreamers to demand the impossible. Founded in 2007 by a small group of people with decades of publishing, media, and organizing experience, we have sold millions of copies of our books, most often one at a time, face to face. We're old enough to know what we're doing and young enough to know what's at stake. Join us to create a better world.

PM Press
PO Box 23912
Oakland, CA 94623
www.pmpress.org

PM Press in Europe
europe@pmpress.org
www.pmpress.org.uk

FRIENDS OF PM PRESS

These are indisputably momentous times—the financial system is melting down globally and the Empire is stumbling. Now more than ever there is a vital need for radical ideas.

In the many years since its founding—and on a mere shoestring—PM Press has risen to the formidable challenge of publishing and distributing knowledge and entertainment for the struggles ahead. With hundreds of releases to date, we have published an impressive and stimulating array of literature, art, music, politics, and culture. Using every available medium, we've succeeded in connecting those hungry for ideas and information to those putting them into practice.

Friends of PM allows you to directly help impact, amplify, and revitalize the discourse and actions of radical writers, filmmakers, and artists. It provides us with a stable foundation from which we can build upon our early successes and provides a much-needed subsidy for the materials that can't necessarily pay their own way. You can help make that happen—and receive every new title automatically delivered to your door once a month—by joining as a Friend of PM Press. And, we'll throw in a free T-shirt when you sign up.

Here are your options:

- **$30 a month** Get all books and pamphlets plus a 50% discount on all webstore purchases
- **$40 a month** Get all PM Press releases (including CDs and DVDs) plus a 50% discount on all webstore purchases
- **$100 a month** Superstar—Everything plus PM merchandise, free downloads, and a 50% discount on all webstore purchases

For those who can't afford $30 or more a month, we have **Sustainer Rates** at $15, $10 and $5. Sustainers get a free PM Press T-shirt and a 50% discount on all purchases from our website.

Your Visa or Mastercard will be billed once a month, until you tell us to stop. Or until our efforts succeed in bringing the revolution around. Or the financial meltdown of Capital makes plastic redundant. Whichever comes first.

Downtown Local

Aaron Cometbus

ISBN: 979-8-88744-109-2
$12.95   128 pages

Tired of handwringing reports about "lost" and "disappearing" New York? These dispatches show a different side of the city—resilient and flourishing despite the naysayers and high rent.

Like a modern-day Joseph Mitchell, Cometbus visits projectionists studying Chinese in their booths, prophets whose pulpits are illegal sublets, and personal assistants who rule the roost once their bosses are out of sight. Readers get a tour of the downtown photographers and the uptown UN missions, complete with a survey of their trash. Punk scientists make their living counting cards at casinos while Albanian waiters keep hidden horseshoe diners open all night. Cover art by Eisner Award winner Nate Powell.

"Aaron crafts evocative essays and concise vignettes that read almost like prose poems."
—New York Press

"A taut and tough delivery that belies the sensibility of a sage."
—Monk